Technology In The Classroom

NATIONAL BUSINESS EDUCATION YEARBOOK, NO. 33

1995

Editor:
NANCY J. GRONEMAN
Emporia State University
Emporia, Kansas

Assistant Editor:
KAREN C. KASER
University of Nebraska-Lincoln
Lincoln, Nebraska

Published by:
National Business Education Association
1914 Association Drive
Reston, Virginia 22091

TECHNOLOGY IN THE CLASSROOM

Copyright 1995

NATIONAL BUSINESS EDUCATION ASSOCIATION
1914 ASSOCIATION DRIVE
RESTON, VIRGINIA

$15

ISBN 0-933964-41-2

Preface

Rapid changes are occurring in the types and uses of technology in classrooms. These new technologies affect both instructional content and instructional delivery methods. Keeping up with these changes can be a daunting task for educators.

Today, all educators must have computer-related skills, but they are becoming overwhelmed with the knowledge they must acquire and skills they must learn in order to stay up to date. The theme for the 1995 NBEA Yearbook, *Technology in the Classroom*, acknowledges that technological skills are essential for all educators. It is hoped that this Yearbook will help educators understand, evaluate, and apply technology in new and effective ways.

The editors recognize that computer technologies change rapidly and that information related to price ranges, hardware capabilities, and software features will change in the future. At the same time, it is important for educators to understand the capabilities and uses for state-of-the-art technology available in 1995.

Designed for use by computer novices and experts, this publication includes basic definitions of new technology in easy-to-understand language, descriptions of software and hardware features and hardware requirements, and examples of practical technology applications for use in classrooms.

The Yearbook is organized into three parts:

Part I: *Technology's Impact on Curricula* addresses the changes in curriculums at all grade levels caused by changes in technology. What has been the effect on course offerings? How is technology used by students? What is the purpose of teaching software to students?

Part II: *Technology as a Teaching Tool* deals with teachers' use of technology to enhance the learning process. In this section, several types of new software programs and technologies are described that can be used by teachers to create instructional presentations or to help them teach students how to locate information at remote sites.

Part III: *Selection and Use of Technology* focuses on criteria for selection of technology, appropriate classroom layouts, and the use of new technologies. Today's educators must have a working knowledge of various operating systems, graphical user environments, computer networks, and other new technologies.

Contributing authors are to be commended for their willingness to share their expertise related to teaching and using the latest technologies on the market. They represent all NBEA regions and a variety of business and business education backgrounds and experiences.

Technology in the Classroom is a refereed yearbook. Chapters were reviewed by at least three persons. Manuscripts for all chapters were divided among members of the NBEA Publications Committee for the first review. Members of the editorial review board were:

Nancy J. Groneman, Editor

Contents

CHAPTER   PAGE

PART I
TECHNOLOGY'S IMPACT ON CURRICULA

1   Technology's Impact on Computer and Business Curricula   1

SUSAN JADERSTROM
Santa Rosa Junior College-Petaluma Center
Petaluma, California

2   Teaching Technology vs. Technology as a Teaching Tool   10

DONNA L. KIZZIER
University of Nebraska-Lincoln
Lincoln, Nebraska

3   The Impact of Technology on Undergraduate
Business Education Preparation Programs: A Model   25

ROGER RANKIN
Idaho State University
Pocatello, Idaho

PART II
TECHNOLOGY AS A TEACHING TOOL

4   Technology and the Development of Critical Thinking Skills   32

B. JUNE SCHMIDT
Virginia Polytechnic Institute and State University
Blacksburg, Virginia

MARGARET STIDHAM KIRBY
Virginia Department of Education
Richmond, Virginia

5   Technical Training Methods   40

BRIDGET N. O'CONNOR
New York University
New York, New York

6   Desktop Presentation Software—What Is It and
How Can It Be Used?   50

PAT R. GRAVES
Eastern Illinois University
Charleston, Illinois

7   Multimedia: An Educational Tool 62

HEIDI R. PERREAULT
Southwest Missouri State University
Springfield, Missouri

8   Electronic Mail, Bulletin Board Systems, Conferences:
Connections for the Electronic Teaching/Learning Age 73

MARIE E. FLATLEY
San Diego State University
San Diego, California

JENNIFER HUNTER
Western Carolina University
Cullowhee, North Carolina

9   Interactive Television in the Classroom 86

PATRICIA SAVAGE
Peabody High School
Peabody, Kansas

PART III
SELECTION AND USE OF TECHNOLOGY

10   Evaluating Instructional Technology for
Classroom Application 95

LISA E. GUELDENZOPH

DAVID J. HYSLOP
Bowling Green State University
Bowling Green, Ohio

11   Redesigning the Classroom To Reflect Technology's impact 106

MARSHA BAYLESS
Steven F. Austin State University
Nacogdoches, Texas

12   Computer Operating Systems and Graphical User
Environments—The State of the Art 117

TERRY D. LUNDGREN
Eastern Illinois University
Charleston, Illinois

13   Computer Network Technology: A Survey of
Basic Components, Configurations, and Benefits of
Local Area Networks 126

DENNIS LABONTY
Utah State University
Logan, Utah

14   **Implementing and Troubleshooting a Classroom LAN** **137**

MARCIA JAMES
University of Wisconsin-Whitewater
Whitewater, Wisconsin

15   **CD-ROM Devices in the Classroom** **148**

KATHI TULLY
Olathe School District
Olathe, Kansas

16   **Implications of Emerging Technologies on**
Business and Computer Instruction **154**

NORMAN A. GARRETT
Eastern Illinois University
Charleston, Illinois

PART 1
TECHNOLOGY'S IMPACT ON CURRICULA

CHAPTER 1

Technology's Impact on Computer and Business Curricula

SUSAN JADERSTROM

Santa Rosa Junior College • Petaluma Center
Petaluma, California

Office automation exploded in business during the early 1980s. Since then, business education curricula and classrooms have changed tremendously. Curricula can no longer focus around the typewriter as a means to produce routine correspondence. Because of technology, the scope of jobs has broadened, responsibilities changed, computer proficiency has become necessary, and communication skills are more important than ever.

This chapter will review curricula changes affecting keyboarding, word processing, office systems, accounting, and computer courses as well as expected changes in the future. Curricula need to change quickly for two reasons: (1) to reflect changes in the workplace and (2) to react to changes in other curricula in grades K-16.

By developing partnerships with local businesses and industries, school personnel will have a better understanding of trends in the business world. Curricula must match the knowledge, skills, and attitudes identified as essential by employers. Just as businesses provide employee retraining, schools must provide incentives for professional development so that business and computer teachers can learn emerging technological concepts and applications and integrate them into the classroom.

Changes in elementary and secondary school curricula involving the use of computers have had and will continue to have a tremendous impact on business and computer curricula. In the past, a mainstay of the secondary education business curriculum has been one or more keyboarding courses. Now, keyboarding has impacted various levels of instruction.

IMPACT OF KEYBOARDING ON THE K-16 CURRICULUM

Debates in the 1980s centered on what level to teach keyboarding and who should teach it. While the ideal curriculum may offer a keyboarding sequence of instruction beginning in the elementary grades and continuing through college, in reality keyboarding is not uniformly taught at any particular level or in any standard length of time. What is agreed upon, however, is that keyboarding should be taught on computers.

Elementary and middle school level. Several states recommend that keyboarding be an integral part of the elementary curriculum. Elementary keyboarding helps students become more efficient at using the computer in the language arts area, enhancing skills such as spelling, vocabulary, and writing. Elementary students can also use science and math programs more productively if they can keyboard.

Occasionally, secondary business teachers teach elementary keyboarding, but they are more likely involved in developing and offering a short in-service program to teach the basic competencies of keyboarding and keyboarding methods to elementary teachers.

Many middle schools (grades 6-8) teach keyboarding in a structured daily class, ranging from six weeks to a semester, taught by a business instructor using tutorial software. Often the class is a combination of keyboarding and computer awareness. The goal of the class is to reinforce prior keyboarding knowledge and to continue emphasizing efficiency at the keyboard through personal-use applications.

Secondary level. Many secondary schools offer courses similar to the middle school level and geared toward all students. The emphasis is on text-entry skills and more efficient use of the computer keyboard. The course combines keyboarding skills with basic word processing skills using industry-standard software.

The next level of keyboarding at the secondary level usually combines skill building and document formatting, using word processing software as a tool to build keyboarding speed and accuracy. Specialized skill-building software is also used, which individualizes drills and timings and keeps a progress record. The emphasis is on creation of business-related documents.

Offering keyboarding instruction in elementary schools may cause several problems for secondary business teachers. First, elementary level keyboarding instruction may have a negative impact on student enrollment in secondary level keyboarding courses. To overcome this problem, secondary business teachers may need to "sell" students on the usefulness of increasing keyboarding speed and accuracy and of learning proper document formats. Second, keyboarding teachers in secondary schools may find it difficult to accommodate the varying abilities of students entering their classes. To help overcome this problem, teachers can use keyboarding software and drill software for remedial work. Software correlated with textbooks that automatically checks timings and documents produced can also be useful.

Two-year colleges and universities. The trend is to combine teaching keyboarding skills with word processing skills using industry-standard software with course names reflecting this trend. Once students have reached basic keyboarding competency, skill development is encouraged by using skill building software. Students are expected to format and produce a variety of business documents using word processing software.

Flexibility in keyboarding instruction is vital at the college level because skills vary so much. Assessment and analysis of skills are important in counseling students and placing them in appropriate courses. Keyboarding is often offered in a variety of formats, ranging from individualized, self-paced programs to traditional, teacher-led classes.

At the university level, basic keyboarding skills are often not taught, but are considered prerequisite skills for word processing and desktop publishing courses.

IMPACT OF WORD PROCESSING ON THE CURRICULUM K-16

Word processing software is the most widely used package in schools, homes, and offices. Word processing has been a part of business education instruction for over a decade and still remains the core of most programs. While word processing has impacted business and computer curricula, it has affected many other curricula as well.

Elementary and middle school. Elementary teachers may have not changed language arts curricula substantially, but they have changed the tools students use to create paragraphs and stories—from paper and pencil to a computer, word processing software, and a printer.

Middle school students use word processing for any written assignments whether they are related to language arts instruction, science, history, or geography.

Elementary and middle school instructors typically teach easy-to-use word processing packages, since the goal is using word processing as a tool for personal use. While sophisticated formatting such as footers may not be used, some word processing programs allow students to insert graphics into documents to create storybooks.

Secondary school. Before using word processing software, high school students must complete basic keyboarding and skill building instruction. At the secondary school level, the word processing package should be one used frequently in business—it should be industry-standard. At this level, students are often introduced to a software package different than the one used in their previous courses so they can become more versatile. Secondary word processing instructors use mailability standards and have students prepare a variety of documents using specialized software functions.

Two-year colleges and universities. Two-year colleges and universities are in a constant state of change in word processing instruction in order to meet the needs of adult students who need training and retraining for business and industry. At this level, curriculum must be totally flexible and offer courses covering many industry-standard word processing packages.

Formats vary from self-paced, short courses to teacher-directed, semester-length courses. Instructional techniques such as audio-visual and computer-assisted instruction are used. Classes are often available on the weekends and during other nontraditional times. These courses appeal to a broad range of students, who have different goals and objectives. Credit/no-credit options become important for people who need the knowledge but do not want to worry about grades.

Students in two-year colleges preparing for employment are encouraged to become proficient in several word processing packages and expert in at least one package. Students are encouraged to learn more than one computer platform to increase their employability. Advanced word processing courses increase student proficiency in adapting software for particular jobs and industries. Students generate complex documents, use desktop publishing features, and import and export information among software packages.

Generally, universities place less emphasis than two-year colleges on offering a variety of word processing courses covering different software packages. Universities place less emphasis on short-term noncredit word processing training than two-year colleges. At the university level, word processing instruction may be included in campus-wide introduction to computer courses or in courses required of Office Systems or Business Education majors. Word processing is often used in English composition classes also.

CHANGES IN OFFICE SYSTEMS COURSES

Because of the increase in technology, curriculum development is complex in the office systems area. While several curriculum models are available from professional associations, adapting them to keep up with the monthly changes in technology can be difficult.

Administrative support workers do most of their work on the computer, completing tasks using desktop publishing, computer graphics, telecommunications software, and local area networks. New software programs and computer-related hardware are coming on the market every month making it difficult for business employees and students to keep up to date.

Students need to be familiar with these various new technologies. However, it is not easy for instructors to learn new software programs yearly and to teach new software when there are no textbooks on the market related to it.

Because of these changes in administrative support worker responsibilities and in technologies, new courses have been developed and integrated into business and computer curricula.

Secondary level. An overview course, sometimes called Business Technologies or Computer Technologies, gives students a foundation in computer applications. This course introduces operating systems, word processing, database, spreadsheets, desktop publishing, multimedia, and telecommunications. A simulation ties all parts of the course together. The difference between this instruction and middle school computer applications courses is that the secondary level course uses industry-standard software and business applications.

A comprehensive technology-based course is replacing the traditional office procedures course. Topics include office health and safety issues, organization and time management, decision making, national and international communications, records management, and telecommunications. Students learn manual procedures in addition to applying technology to a wide range of business problems. This course is often called Administrative Support and Procedures or Administrative Procedures and Technologies. It is taught on both the secondary and two-year college levels.

Two-year colleges and universities. Besides the major change in office procedures described above, colleges and universities are also adding new courses to the curriculum. Because of the increase in local area networks and the wide variety of communications tools now available in offices, a telecommunications course is important. This course covers communicating using facsimile and fax boards, accessing electronic bulletin boards, using an online database to research information, communicating effectively using electronic mail, and understanding the concepts of a local area network.

An operating systems course is a basis for all software applications courses at the college level. This course provides training in using computers to work with utilities at the operating system level. The utility system taught is usually dependent on the most popular operating system in the local community.

The office supervision course now emphasizes supervising people and technology. This course is designed around the skills necessary for managing a diverse workforce and the technology and resources necessary to productively accomplish office tasks. Students use management software such as project managers, budgeting, presentations, and personal information managers.

Besides desktop publishing, new courses are being offered in business graphics and fundamentals of design. In these courses students become familiar with graphic design techniques and principles of page layout. Students use a variety of graphics software packages to plan, design, and produce attractive documents and publications.

Presentation media is an advanced course offered after students are proficient in word processing. This course acquaints students with the development and production of professional presentation materials, including overhead transparencies, slide presentations, computer-projected presentations, and multimedia presentations.

CHANGES IN THE ACCOUNTING CURRICULUM

Of all the areas of business that use computers, none relies on them more heavily than finance and accounting departments. The biggest change in the accounting curricula, on both the secondary and postsecondary levels, has been the integration of computer software. Some instructors are teaching less theory in order to have time to integrate computerized accounting into courses.

Secondary level. On the secondary level, instructors usually use an educational accounting software program and simulations throughout the traditional accounting course. This educational software is similar to commercial accounting software but is not as complex, is easier for students to use, and is designed as a teaching tool. Capstone experiences include completing simulations using software. Advanced students use industry-standard accounting software packages and spreadsheet software.

Two-year colleges and universities. At the two-year college level students use industry-standard accounting software packages, based on local and statewide needs assessments, as soon as fundamental accounting principles have been covered. College textbooks are available to help teach this integrated microcomputer approach to accounting so instructors do not have to develop their own computer instructions.

Students are expected to be proficient using several top spreadsheet programs on the market and become expert with one of the software packages. Students enter data, complete analyses, and create custom reports.

Businesses often ask two-year colleges for short training classes in a specific kind of accounting software package. These courses are designed for individuals who have a working knowledge of accounting but who need the computerized concepts and special functions. These courses are often offered on the weekends or at the employer's place of business.

Advanced accounting and specialty accounting courses (cost accounting, income tax accounting, and managerial accounting) use spreadsheets and their graphing capabilities for summarizing and analyzing data. Specific software packages are used as much as possible, such as income tax software in the income tax accounting course.

At the university level the lowest level accounting course may be required of all business majors. While the content of the course has changed from an emphasis on entering transactions to a managerial approach, entering transactions is still a substantial part of this course. The use of accounting software can easily be integrated into the instruction.

In higher level accounting courses, spreadsheet software, accounting software with advanced auditing capabilities, and statistics software programs are often used by students as tools to complete assignments.

CHANGES IN THE COMPUTER CURRICULUM

Computer knowledge has now merged with general literacy. Computer courses used to be clearly defined as programming courses where students wrote programs line by line. Automatic code generation reduced the need for pure programmers. Employers now look for computer specialists with business expertise, combining business analysis with programming skills.

Computer instructors traditionally taught computer history/literacy. For the most part, history of computers is relegated to an appendix or perhaps one chapter in a textbook. Computer literacy today focuses on how computers are used in specific fields such as law, government, manufacturing, or art. Emphasis is on understanding the operating systems and software.

Middle school. Computer literacy is now taught at the middle school level. The course content covers understanding the basic functions and operations of computers, computers' effect on society, and the use of a variety of computer software programs as tools for communicating and learning. The computer literacy course sometimes includes a keyboarding instruction unit.

Secondary level. Some secondary schools are still teaching computer programming, but the emphasis today has shifted toward a basic understanding of a variety of software packages and operating systems. Most schools offer a general course that introduces operating systems, word processing, database, spreadsheets, desktop publishing, and telecommunications.

Also available in many schools are advanced courses on a variety of software packages. Students use industry-standard software and produce documents typically found in businesses. Instructors expect students to think analytically, manipulate information, and use the computer as a productivity tool.

Two-year colleges and universities. Nearly all two-year colleges offer computer applications courses such as introduction to computers, operating systems, word processing, database, spreadsheets, desktop publishing, and telecommunications.

These courses are offered in a variety of flexible formats to meet the goals of a wide range of students. Often a student can obtain a year or more of instruction in a specific software package and become extremely proficient in adapting and using that package for completing business applications.

Computer-related certificate and degree programs at two-year colleges prepare students for basic programming jobs and for jobs in computer maintenance, operations, and user support. In these programs, students learn the following:

- programming languages
- installing computer hardware
- selecting, operating, and managing computer networks
- selecting, installing, and evaluating appropriate software for business situations
- prioritizing, analyzing, and troubleshooting computer problems.

Students are also trained to assemble the most efficient system for the user or become LAN (Local area network) managers and maintain LANs.

Training in information and image management is a recent course added to college curricula because of demand for background in imaging. Imaging is becoming standard practice for financial services, insurance, accounting firms, and other organizations that must store massive amounts of written materials. Students trained in this area help install imaging systems that can scan documents into the computer and then help check them for accuracy. Imaging is also a subject being integrated into records management courses.

Another course recently added to the college curriculum is multimedia. Students get experience combining text, graphics, music, voice, and video media. Students usually need some background in programming, graphics, and design.

Universities offer degrees for programmers, but the many technological innovations in programming have redefined the role of the programmer and led to new skill requirements. Instead of having a mathematical or engineering background, programmers are expected to have computer expertise and the ability to combine business analysis with programming skills. Progamming languages such as C language have replaced some of the languages of the 1970s and 1980s.

University-level degree programs that prepare systems analysts, who design the system that decides what code the programmer will need to write, have also changed. Courses now teach students how to evaluate the needs of departments and individuals and see what improvements they can make to meet changing business requirements.

Education for the system integrator involves learning many skills of technicians such as installing computers and networks. Courses also teach a high level of software knowledge and expertise with specialized hardware devices that connect networks including gateways and routers. The system integrator is trained to assemble the most efficient system for the user.

EXPECTED CHANGES IN CURRICULA IN THE NEXT FIVE YEARS

Computers will become an increasingly important part of our lives. Few careers will involve computers more than those in the field of business. In addition, skills described as essential today could be completely redefined in as little as four or five years.

In the future we will see technological breakthroughs in artificial intelligence, voice recognition, and virtual reality that will make those technologies useful rather than experimental. The keyboard will no longer be the primary input device for computers. Electronic mail will become the primary form of internal communication. Computer programs will be easier to customize to suit personal needs, likes, and dislikes.

Students must be taught to adapt quickly to change and to keep up with the latest innovations and methods through retraining. Technology should be a part of every class. Students should be encouraged to learn everything they can about technology, which will make them more marketable when looking for a job. Expertise in technology will contribute to their future mobility, advancement potential, compensation, and job satisfaction.

Instructors must constantly be reviewing their instructional goals and strategies to prepare students for the changing workplace. Business educators will need to be futurists to anticipate technological change and translate that knowledge into proactive curriculum planning and implementation. Teachers will need to be adaptable, flexible, and willing to change curriculum quickly and often. Learning new hardware and software is an on-going process. The role of the instructor is changing; he or she is becoming a facilitator of learning, encouraging students to explore and learn through discovery.

With limited funding, business and computer departments may find it difficult to stay up to date, let alone be proactive. Common sense in technology selection must prevail. The cost of equipment needs to be considered in relation to its immediate value. Some technologies, such as facsimiles, affect many people, but the training time is negligible. Voice recognition software was available before 1992, but until it has been perfected and is being accepted in the business world, it may not be useful to invest in voice recognition equipment. History shows that technology costs usually drop by 50 percent or more within a year after being on the market. Sometimes technology costs must be balanced against the need to stay on the cutting edge of technology.

Other constraints affect university-level course offerings also. Limited faculty resources mean that fewer and fewer courses can be offered. Technologies may need to be integrated into existing courses. This may mean the integration of word processing, electronic mail, and desktop presentation software in business communication classes and the integration of spreadsheets in accounting classes. Some technology courses may need to be combined, such as an advanced word processing course and a desktop publishing course.

Today, it is more important than ever to establish partnerships with businesses and industry. To justify requests for new technologies, business and computer educators need the support of business representatives who are on advisory councils.

Business and computer educators must know the new procedures occurring in offices and translate those procedures into appropriate learning activities. It is also important to establish partnerships with other educators, since many careers, although not directly related to computers, rely heavily on them. As long as business enrollments plummet in universities, business educators must take the leadership role in forming these linkages with others and developing courses to meet the needs of a wide variety of students.

SUMMARY

Computers continue to be an integral part of business education curricula and have caused course changes at all levels of education, from elementary school through university levels. Course content needs to be continually reviewed and evaluated to ensure it is meeting the needs of students who will be going into the workforce or continuing their education. Business educators cannot work in isolation but must form partnerships with businesses and other instructors to provide sequenced, collaborative programs. The challenge is for business educators to keep current and be comfortable with their changing role as facilitators of learning.

CHAPTER 2

Teaching Technology vs. Technology as a Teaching Tool

DONNA L. KIZZIER

University of Nebraska-Lincoln, Lincoln, Nebraska

In 1892, at the Worlds' Columbia Exposition in Chicago, the introduction of two technologies altered the future of the world. Futurists conjectured the extent to which the technologies would affect life in the next century, predicting that every American village would have at least one telephone by the year 2000 and that motion pictures would be a benefit to teachers. No one predicted the profound effect telephone technology would have on business, science, social, and educational institutions, nor did anyone foresee the importance of motion pictures in the entertainment industry.

Over a century later, the world is being transformed by information and educational technologies that rival the effect of the phone and the motion picture. Once again, futurists predict revolutionary applications for such powerful technologies as the global information highway, multimedia, distance learning, decision support systems, and expert systems.

Few doubt that these and other technologies will have a dramatic impact on how we conduct business and deliver education. The real effect, however, may not be fully realized for another century, when our ancestors will look back on ways we applied today's technological innovations. How we use technology in education is limited only by our imaginations; what we use is limited by our resourcefulness.

This chapter discusses technological use in educational settings from two perspectives: (1) teaching the technology and (2) using technology as a teaching or learning tool.

DEFINITIONS

Teaching the technology. Business teachers have served as both pioneers and leaders in "teaching the technology." In this role, teachers prepare students with the competencies to productively use current business hardware and software. Business and computer teachers have done a superb job teaching word processing, spreadsheet, database, graphics, desktop publishing, and other software programs.

As the use of information technology has exploded in the business world, educators have scrambled to add relevant competencies to the curriculum, adding such state-of-the-art technology as networks, communications tools, scanners, facsimile, and multimedia.

Technology as a teaching tool. In addition to teaching technology, educators use technology as a teaching tool. In addition to teaching students how to use business information technologies, teachers use information and educational technologies as teaching tools. Technology as a teaching tool is used in one of two ways: (1) Students use the technology as a vehicle to learn skills and concepts beyond the technology itself, or (2) the teacher uses technology to enhance or support teaching.

COMPARISON OF THE VALUE OF EACH APPROACH

Each approach is appropriately used and necessary for the curriculum. Although a distinction is being drawn between teaching technology and using technology as a teaching tool for the purposes of this chapter, it is often difficult to distinguish which competencies are taught through the teaching technology approach and which are gained through learners using technology as a teaching tool.

To illustrate how these two approaches can become inextricably interwoven, an example is offered in preparing students to navigate the information resources available on Internet. Using online documentation and interactive training technology, some students may gain necessary Internet competencies without a "formal" training session. This stage illustrates teaching technology even though a human teacher was not present.

After students acquire necessary Internet competencies, the instructor can use Internet technology as a teaching tool. The same students might use Internet to conduct research by accessing school libraries, communicate online with experts worldwide, and transmit progress reports to the instructor for interactive feedback. In conducting these tasks, both the students and the instructor are using technology as a teaching/learning tool.

As students feel more confident with their newly found Internet navigational skills, the learners may go back to the online documentation and interactive training tools to learn more about Internet before pursuing the next assignment, beginning the cycle from teaching technology to technology as a teaching tool once again.

The previous example illustrates the sometimes fuzzy line between teaching technology and technology as a teaching tool. This line is expected to become fuzzier as educators move more toward a "learning by doing" or "training on demand" model in which students learn skills and knowledge as they need them to complete projects and assignments. However, this method of instruction may not be the most efficient or effective. Students may learn word processing features from English teachers and spreadsheets from science teachers. The teachers may not have the depth of knowledge or skills themselves.

With the growth of educational technology, this customized approach to education is a reality in some educational settings. For example, electronic performance support systems (EPSS), which provide training on demand through dynamic multimedia dialogue with learners at their work stations, are winning a small, growing, and passionate following in the corporate community.

Although the learning-by-demand learning model is a different educational framework than what most educators are accustomed to, the fact that learners must first learn the technology before they use it as a tool will not change. What will change are the delivery options available to students to learn the technologies. While the use of EPSSs is a sophisticated example of technology as a teaching tool, the skills and knowledge taught by the educational technology is still an example of teaching technology. Technology simply increases the options available to the instructor for delivering instruction to the learner.

As technology becomes more widespread in schools and models of learning adapt to the more student-directed approach, the lines between teaching technology and technology as a teaching tool will continue to become even more blurred. Even though each approach is often closely interwoven in the learning process, it is important to recognize the value of both approaches to the learner.

Business, computer, and other teachers are beginning to create instructional materials using presentation graphics software and hypermedia software as teaching tools. With these programs, teachers can create visually attractive transparencies or slides, automated computer presentations with sound and animation, or interactive hypermedia presentations.

EVOLUTION OF TECHNOLOGY IN EDUCATION

Since the application of motion picture technology in educational settings a hundred years ago, technology has provided teachers with increasingly powerful tools to enrich the learning environment. Not only are new technologies being developed, but old educational technologies, such as videotape and overhead devices, are being integrated with powerful information technologies.

Business and computer educators have played a unique role in the application of both educational and information technologies in that they not only use educational technology, but they also have served as leaders in teaching information technologies. This leadership role continues as business educators are called upon to collaborate in the planning and implementation of technologies within educational settings. The brief history that follows summarizes the evolution of how information technology has been applied in educational settings.

In the 1960s and 1970s, the use of information technology in schools was primarily used in two ways: (1) to teach third generation programming languages, such as BASIC, FORTRAN or COBOL; and (2) as a content delivery device to deliver computer-assisted instruction, simulations, tutorials, educational games, and the like.

During the 1980s, teaching students about technology (computer literacy) as well as how to use popular computer applications was widespread. During this decade, information technology increasingly began to be used as a learning and thinking tool. The tools incorporated critical thinking, problem solving, decision making, creativity, and exploration. During this time, such applications as word processing, database, spreadsheet, telecommunications, graphing, desktop publishing, and hypermedia were popular.

In the later part of the 1980s and into the 1990s, technology was increasingly applied as a teaching tool. For example, the technology enabled such applications as: small groups working together using group decision support systems; using computers as electronic chalkboards; using telecommunications and distance learning technologies to reach beyond the physical walls of the classroom; personalizing technology to students' individual needs, styles, and goals, enabling student-directed learning; and adding realism through such technologies as multimedia, hypertext, and optical disc.

As the evolution continues, educators are developing creative applications for emerging technologies. The next section discusses some of the ways educators are using some of these exciting new technologies.

IDENTIFICATION OF PROCESSES FOR EACH APPROACH

As was true a century ago, the best minds still cannot envision all the potential uses for today's dizzying array of sophisticated information and educational technology. Educators are just beginning to explore the horizons of potential applications. The difference is not so much in the technologies themselves as in educators' imagining how those technologies can be employed.

The listing which follows defines numerous technologies and suggests examples of how each can be used within the teaching technology and technology-as-an-instructional tool approaches. Examples are denoted using the following abbreviations:

TT   Teach the Technology

IT   Use Technology as an Instructional Tool

The listing and accompanying examples, placed in alphabetic order for easier reference, are not meant to be exhaustive, but rather illustrative of ways educators have found to employ a variety of emerging educational and information technologies.

Adaptive technology: Hardware/software for special needs learners

IT   Special needs learners interact with software by using such devices as vertical keyboards, software to adapt the keyboard for one-handed typists and enlarge print for visually impaired learners. In addition, such input devices as headsets and foot pedals are available through adaptive technologies to adapt to users' special needs.

Artificial intelligence/expert systems: A technology which mimics human thought processes and reasoning.

TT   Courses in fifth generation programming using expert systems are taught at collegiate levels and are beginning to be offered within high school curricula. For example, the Classical Greek Magnet High School in Kansas City, Missouri, offers a natural language processing and expert systems course.

IT   Courses designed using artificial intelligence/expert systems can be designed to accommodate learners diverse learning styles, resulting in customized instruction for each individual. For example, a course using an expert system was designed by a University of Central Florida accounting teacher to teach the basic techniques of accounting. The system integrates the accumulated knowledge of the discipline to engage students in its mastery. The tool serves as a customized review and assessment tool.

Automated phone systems: Sophisticated audio technologies which receive, store, retrieve, and distribute voice messages.

IT Automated notification systems are being used by schools to deliver messages to customized lists of students, parents, and other constituency groups. At Harkers Island, North Carolina, parents leave voice mail for specific teachers and access a phone-in homework and activity hotline daily. At Harkers, overall attendance increased, with at-risk student attendance increasing significantly. Some sites also reported dramatic increases in parent-teacher interaction increasing with voice mail.

K-8 schools in Billings, Montana, installed phone and voice mail systems in all classrooms in 1992, allowing students to call parents during the day to report good news and to speak via speaker phone with such personalities as President Clinton.

Bar code scanners: Input device used to pre-program access to CDs and laser discs

IT Generally used for whole class instruction, bar code scanners are increasingly bundled with combination videotape, CD/laser disc devices. Publishing companies provide bar-code and laser discs within textbook support materials to allow the instructor to access powerful video material to illustrate specific points. For example, in a unit on economics, economists discussing counterpoint ideas could be presented and then discussed.

Computer assisted design (CAD): Software that allows design engineers to simulate the effect of various options on ergonomic factors.

TT Within information systems or industrial technology courses, students are taught how to use the software for relevant applications.

IT As part of a class project in which office ergonomics is studied, students use CAD to design proposed office environments for a case study site. The study might be done in conjunction with students from the industrial technology drafting program.

CD-ROM: A 4¾-inch optical disc that can store text, sound, and video. It is used with PC technology as a high-density random storage device.

TT Students are taught how to access CD-ROM library databases to conduct research and to record data and audio on CDs for student presentations.

IT Teachers use CD-ROMs to design audiovisual class presentations.

Students use CD-ROM resources to conduct research and to facilitate preparation of reports for class presentations.

Desktop publishing: Use of a PC and software to prepare printed materials having different type styles, sizes, and formats.

TT   Students are taught how to use desktop publishing software and desktop publishing features of sophisticated word processing software.

IT   Students use desktop publishing to create materials for student projects while teachers create newsletters, transparencies, flyers, and slides.

Distance learning: Schools and businesses use instructional technology to deliver instruction, software, and library resources outside the walls of the classroom.

TT   Students and teachers learn how to effectively use such distance learning technology as videoconferencing, electronic chalkboards, one and two-way audio, one and two-way video, facsimile, 800 numbers, and high resolution TV monitors. Teachers learn effective interactive strategies to teach and support instruction using distance technology.

IT   Teachers use distance learning technology to deliver instruction to remote classrooms, possibly across the world. Course offerings are expanded without having to duplicate expertise at each institution. For example, in western Nebraska, a multi-point compressed video class using 800 numbers allows instructors to teach from sick beds and students to participate in class by calling from hotel lobbies, offices, and restaurants. Using NebSat and CorpNet in Nebraska, Spanish and college English courses are delivered from Sutherland, Nebraska, to Callaway, Wallace, and Austin, Pennsylvania, using two-way audio and an electronic chalkboard. Also in Nebraska, human relations courses needed for teacher certification are offered from a western state college to four remote western locations.

Students call in, using 800 numbers, to ask questions of the instructor or teaching assistants.

Electronic gradebooks: Software that stores, calculates, analyzes, and prints grade reports.

TT   Pre-service and in-service teachers learn how to use electronic gradebooks.

IT   Teachers use electronic gradebooks to store grades, weigh them, convert to letter grades, and print reports for students, parents, and administrators.

Electronic mail: A system that allows electronic message and document transfer without the need to physically transfer paper.

TT   Students learn how to use such electronic mail systems.

IT   Teachers use an electronic mail system to conveniently communicate in a timely and inexpensive manner with students, colleagues, and content experts and to review students' work and to provide feedback.

Students use electronic mail systems to communicate in a timely and inexpensive manner with other students and with faculty and content experts. Students can transmit work to instructors and receive feedback.

Electronic performance support systems (EPSS): Electronic systems that support the user in achieving a performance objective; the EPSS may incorporate expert systems that help solve problems; knowledge bases; a user interface for communication; productivity software; help systems that give explanations, demonstrations, advice, and alternatives for systems operation; assessment systems to evaluate knowledge or skill; and feedback systems to tell users about appropriateness of their actions. The system lets learners decide how and when they will learn.

TT   Learners are trained in how to use the system and can take technological training courses on the system.

IT   Instructors become designers and facilitators, selecting appropriate materials to place on the system and supporting learners.

Ongoing testing is embedded in the system, as is translation and adaptation to various work or learning cultures and accommodation for various learning styles. This system is ideal for environments in which students are empowered with self-directed learning.

For example, Steelcase employees schedule their own training through the firm's electronic mail system; then using the EPSS to determine their personal learning styles, they match their styles with course materials from a list of 260 training options and use the system's self-assessment testing function to monitor their progress. IBM is instituting EPS systems in place of formal classroom courses, organizing it around skills needed rather than jobs.

Electronic tablets: An electronic device placed on top of an LCD projection panel that lets users write comments or add emphasis to computer information presented via the panel.

TT   The proper use of the technology, such as how to select colors and symbols, can be taught.

IT   Teachers can display examples of computer applications and use the electronic table as one would use an overhead pen on a transparency, illustrating major points. The device, using the blank page format, can also be used like a chalkboard without affecting materials being presented.

Learners can use the tablet to emphasize presentations they make for class projects.

Facsimile: An electronic device that transmits images rather than voice, data, or video.

TT   Students can learn how to use the technology within standalone machines or on boards within microcomputers.

IT   Instructors and students can use facsimile to transmit images to each other; often used as a support technology in distance learning environments.

Graphics tablets: An electronic device that allows input of artistic work, similar to drawing with a pen.

TT   Students can learn how to use tablets as input devices.

IT   Teachers and students can enhance their presentations by creating artistic drawings not available within clip art.

Group support systems (GSS): Software that enables group participants on a network to participate in a variety of group decision-making activities. Each participant keyboards responses for display on a public screen. The system is designed to clarify the thinking process in problem solving.

TT   Students learn how to operate the groupware system, i.e., the network, public screen, and GSS software functions.

IT   The GSS can be effective for teaching students how to use a variety of group strategies such as brainstorming, customer needs assessment, market research, group conferencing, idea organization, and policy formation. Also, it prepares students to structure effective teamwork, to set up agendas, to create order out of chaos, and to work collaboratively in teams. In the classroom, GSS can be effective in case study situations and to support collaborative and distance learning.

Student teams can use GSS to enhance decision making, vision, and creativity. The negatives associated with group work can be eliminated, such as conformance pressure, socializing, forgetting others' responses, lack of focus on issues, slow feedback, and nonparticipation. The system can be tied to multimedia to provide information on demand to support decision making.

Hypermedia: A technology that combines the information storage and retrieval aspects of hyperlinking technology, which mimics the human thought process.

TT   Students can be taught how to use hypermedia tools to create interactive multimedia presentations that combine text, sound, scanned pictures, graphics, buttons, and animation.

IT   Instructors can design hypermedia applications as intuitive on-line tutorials for students or to create multimedia or interactive video presentations.

Learners can use hypermedia applications for on-line help on completing assignments. Students can share their hypermedia files with other students, thus creating libraries on topics of interest. Proponents suggest that hypermedia stimulates users' interest in assignments and aids in the learning process. Such multimedia elements as pictures, video, sound, and diagrams are used.

I-mail: Using computers to electronically copy, store, transmit, and retrieve visuals, graphics, and documents containing text.

TT   Users can be taught to use I-mail functions.

IT   Teachers can use the system to call up students' assignments which were faxed to the instructor's computer and to return them by fax without printing. Teachers and students can annotate materials by writing or by voice annotation. As technology advances it is predicted that teachers can provide class materials in the form of interactive audio and video.

Students can fax assignments to the instructor's computer and receive a response by return fax (without printing). In the future, students will be able to "remotely attend class" with fully interactive audio and video computer capabilities.

Information highway: The ability to search remote libraries, communicate worldwide, engage in wide-ranging topics, and access resources. For example, Internet (the international high performance communication network) provides high speed communication among two million computers and 20 million users located in 125 countries on seven continents.

TT   Teachers can instruct students on how to use communication, research, and file transfer resources on Internet.

IT   Instructors can download programs, data, and even visual files to prepare multimedia presentations, talk to experts worldwide about subjects of interest, and tap information from resources to aid their teaching and research.

Students can get career and college/university information online, engage experts and other students worldwide about subjects of interest, search remote libraries, send messages to instructors and other students,

Integrated software: Software that combines word processing, database, and spreadsheet functions, among other options.

TT   Students are taught how to operate the various software packages and how to integrate data into the various functions. Such functions as graphics, thesaurus, foreign word dictionaries, and desktop publishing functions are often included.

IT   Teachers can use integrated software to create mailing labels for notes to parents, to update student records on the database, to calculate grades on the spreadsheet, and to write documents on the word processing system.

Students use integrated software to complete projects for information systems classes and then use their new skills to support work for other classes.

Interactive books: A technology that teams text and illustrations with dramatic narration, music, and sound effects, plus a full set of reading and learning tools.

TT   Users can be instructed on how to use interactive books.

IT   Interactive books can be used for whole-group instruction to bring concepts to life.

Learners can use interactive books individually to direct their own instruction. Many interactive books automatically translate to a foreign language and provide explanations of words, etc. These books can be used to teach students whose second language is English.

Interactive video technology: The placement of a small video camera on a computer to videotape trainees as they practice skills. Trainees play back their videotaped performance and compare their competence with a pre-recorded expert; this strategy is called "shaping-prompting." QuickTime and Hypercard are some of the potential underlying technologies used.

IT   The teacher can use authoring tools to design the instruction.

A learner sits at the computer system, watching a pre-recorded expert demonstrate a skill, such as teaching, counseling, selling, public speaking, leadership, customer service, or operation of a technical piece of equipment. The learners then attempt to perform the same skill, in real time and motion, emulating the expert while being recorded by the video camera. The computer then plays back the learner's performance on one half of the screen and the expert's performance on the other half of the screen so the learner can compare the two performances.

Multimedia: A technology that combines television quality, full-motion video, analog audio, digital audio, text, and graphics, using both laser disc and CD-ROM.

TT   Students can be trained in the use of multimedia to prepare projects and presentations.

IT   Teachers use multimedia to teach difficult concepts. For example, students can analyze situations to challenge their attitudes about diversity, tolerance, and sensitivity by working interactively with various scenarios on videodisc. Or, students can focus on decision-making and self-management techniques and the resultant consequences by working through work scenarios.

Students can access information on multimedia encyclopedias or take courses independently by using multimedia courseware. For example, Federal Express uses multimedia courseware to train customer-contact employees about the proper use of forms.

Operating systems/environments/user interfaces: Software with which the end-user interacts to provide a more intuitive, friendly, and transparent access to computer application software.

TT   Learners develop skills to use various operating systems, environments, and user interfaces such as DOS, Macintosh, and Windows.

IT   The teacher tailors the technology to individual learning styles to increase learning effectiveness. The teacher might, for example, set up special icons for various courses using Windows or configure a local area network menu to be more friendly for learners.

Presentation software: Software that allows users to organize ideas, import graphics, text, video, and clip art.

TT   Students are taught how to use the various functions of the software.

IT   Teachers can create large group presentations that "come alive" and provide exciting opportunities for students to interact. For example, after discussing the effects of new tax regulations, actual graphs can be displayed showing those effects.

Students can present reports using presentation software.

Projection systems: A device which projects images from computer programs, videodiscs, videotapes, and satellite programs. Their sophistication ranges from color LCD to CRT-based and theatre-type projection units. Some systems have built-in hard disks to save images.

TT   Instructors can demonstrate software as well as project images from a variety of storage devices. Projection systems are invaluable in teaching various software packages in whole-class situations, enabling students to compare their screen images with the one on the projection unit. Projection systems can be used in conjunction with a computer system to project lecture/discussion notes or to record main points of a discussion point.

IT   Students can use the projection system to share a variety of media images in presentations with the class.

Reading machines: Combines optical character recognition with a voice synthesizer to scan and recognize text from documents, books, or electronic fax files and then read text aloud to users in multiple languages.

TT   Students can be taught how to operate the machine.

IT   Visually impaired students can use the machine for independent learning, freeing the instructor's time.

Scanners: An input device that is used to digitize data and images.

TT   Students can be taught how to operate various types of scanners such as handheld and flatbed. They can be taught how to incorporate scanned images into desktop publishing documents and presentations created with presentation software.

IT   Teachers can scan images for transparencies, handouts, brochures, or newsletters while students can use scanners to create brochures and flyers for student organizations and class projects.

Translation programs: Software that translates from one language to another.

TT   Students can learn how to use the software to translate correspondence, reports, and other documents.

IT   Teachers can use the program to improve communication with non-English speaking parents or to facilitate communication with English as a second-language students.

TV-Computer: A technology that enables cable TV to be viewed on a screen attached to a computer.

TT   Students can be taught how to toggle from TV to computer.

IT   Enhances capability for individualization. Some students can watch a teleconference via cable TV while others can be accessing information from a CD player attached to the computer.

Videotex: An interactive communication technology that allows users to receive information from and interact with information bases through a television receiver and network technology.

TT   Students and parents can be trained on how to use the system.

IT   At McMillan Junior High in Omaha, Nebraska, weekly student grade reports can be accessed on the system by parents. Students, parents, and teachers communicate on the system, leaving messages. For example, assignments and reminders are sent to students, and parent-teacher conferences are conducted without parents' leaving their homes. McMillan reported great parent involvement, enhancing students' relationships with parents and teachers.

Student teams can complete team assignments without leaving their homes. Students can access lunch menus and school calendars, write contracts, receive school assignments, and complete homework. Students can access bulletin boards, use electronic mail, or conduct live conversation (chat). At McMillan, shy and depressed students opened up to teachers. Student retention, self-esteem, attitude, and achievement improved with under-privileged students.

Visual visualizer: Combines a compact CCD video pickup camera with an overhead projector to display 3-D objects as well as various visuals. Images can be saved to a VCR and displayed on a video monitor, projector, or teleconferencing system.

TT   Students and instructors can be taught to use the full capabilities of the system to display three-dimensional objects, slides, transparencies, print materials, and computer screens.

IT   Students and instructors can use the visual visualizer to enhance their classroom presentations.

Videoconferencing: Technology that allows full video and audio interaction among participants at many sites.

TT   Pre-service and in-service teachers can be taught how to use the technology to control multiple classrooms at various sites.

IT   K-12 teachers can access distance learning networks that colleges and universities are building. Experts can be brought into the classroom from around the world to interact in real-time with students. For example, students dispersed across hundreds of miles on Alaska's North Slope, above the Arctic Circle, learn math and art along with other students, allowing equitable delivery of courses.

Virtual reality: An emerging technology that allows the user to experience full, three-dimensional motion in 360 degrees.

TT   Teachers and students learn how to use virtual reality systems, i.e., how to set up virtual reality laboratories, how to interconnect such user input/output devices as pressure sensitive/sensor gloves, body suits to sense movement, and helmets with motion sensors.

IT   Instructors can use virtual reality to provide the ultimate in student immersion and interaction, tapping students' senses of sight, hearing, touch and kinesthetic senses as well as full interactivity as the student moves in a virtual world.

This emerging technology will most likely be used where training would be expensive or dangerous; for example, to train pilots, employees who work with dangerous or hazardous materials, or astronauts.

Learners could immerse themselves in their learning environment using virtual reality technology; for example, they could converse with a famous person in history or try their hand in acting out a famous event. In group training, team members might actually "walk around" in interpersonal space, "feel the texture" of their feedback to a work group or "hear" an idea taking shape. Work is being conducted for such Virtual Reality models of organizations by Bradford Smith and Charles Grantham at the University of San Francisco.

Voice input/recognition: An input device that allows users to teach their PC to respond to spoken commands.

TT   Students learn how to use the voice input device in conjunction with the keyboard and trackball or mouse.

IT   Teachers can use voice input during whole class presentations by giving verbal commands to the system rather than selecting icons or menu items with a mouse or the keyboard.

Voice input allows students with special physical needs to more easily use information technology.

IMPACT OF USING TECHNOLOGY AS A TEACHING TOOL

Educators are offered a tremendous opportunity as well as a challenge to discover ways to effectively employ this vast array of complex technology. Given their unique history in technological leadership, business and computer educators will most likely play a pivotal role in applying these technologies to help springboard education into the next century. As a result of the revolutionary changes caused by technology, the following implications are envisioned:

1. Technology will empower learners to be lifelong masters of their learning.
2. Technology will enable the teacher's role to shift from that of a "knowledge dispenser" to "learning facilitator."
3. A new breed of educational technology support personnel will evolve, assisting teachers and students with the development and effective use of new technologies.
4. The technology will liberate students and instructors to explore previously untapped worlds of information both inside and outside traditional classroom walls. Learning will become more relevant and stimulating.

5. Given the tremendous commitment of resources to implement sophisticated integrated technologies, educators will need more than ever to develop alliances with other educational institutions, practitioners, and corporate sponsors.

6. Schools will need to make strategic plans to implement the technological infrastructure to deliver integrated technologies.

7. Teacher in-service training and completion of high-quality advanced degrees will be possible at remote school sites.

8. Collaboration and communication will be greatly enhanced among groups concerned with education. Parents, community members, business people, and other educational institutions will be more closely connected with learners, teachers, and the entire educational process.

9. As teachers and learners have become more experienced using technology as a tool, technology will become a vehicle for widespread educational reform.

For business education in particular, the following implications are offered:

1. With the shift from teacher-directed to student-directed learning, a new breed of teacher will be needed in business education, one who is not only technologically sophisticated, but also trained to design and effectively use such technological teaching strategies as multimedia and distance education.

2. Business educators should use their unique background in technology to foster effective and creative uses of technology across the curriculum.

3. With their background of leadership in using, planning, and implementing technology, business educators will continue to play a key role in technological planning and implementation.

What was true 100 years ago still rings true. As technologically savvy as we have become, we still cannot anticipate the full value and complexities of emerging technologies until we explore their potential. The literature is full of examples of schools that are applying sophisticated state-of-the-art technology today. Machiavelli once said, " . . . there is nothing more difficult to take in hand, more perilous to conduct, or more uncertain in its success than to take the lead in the introduction of a new order of things." We are now in the midst of the introduction of the new order; the challenge and opportunity for business educators is to use their unique technological background and leadership skills to facilitate the change process.

REFERENCES

Albright, R. C., and Post, P. E. (August 1993). The challenges of electronic learning. *Training & Development* 47:8; pp. 27-29.

Automated phone system keeps parents, teachers & kids informed. (April 1993). *Technological Horizons in Education (T.H.E.) Journal* 20:9; pp. 50-51.

Carr, C. (October 1992). Is virtual reality virtually here? *Training & Development* 46:10; pp. 37-41.

Fogarty, T. J.; and Goldwater, P. M. (October 1993). An expert system for accounting education." *Technological Horizons in Education (T.H.E.) Journal* 21:3; pp 89-91.

Galagan, P. (March 1994). Think performance, a conversation with Gloria Gery. *Training & Development* 48:3; pp. 47-51.

Heier, J.; Cooley, Van; and Reitz, R. (May 1993). American school 2000: Westfield's technology initiative. *Technological Horizons in Education (T.H.E.) Journal* 20:10; pp. 83-86.

Ladd, C. (August 1993). Should performance support be in your computer? *Training & Development* 47:8; pp. 22-24, 26.

The role of technology in business education. (October 1992). *Business Education Forum* 47:1; pp. 15-16.

Videoconferencing bridges gaps in distance and curriculum for Alaskan students. (April 1993). *Technological Horizons in Education (T.H.E.) Journal* 20:9; p. 34.

Wess, R. G. (April 1993). Distance learning options available in western Nebraska. *Technological Horizons in Education (T.H.E.) Journal* 20:9; pp. 62-67.

CHAPTER 3

The Impact of Technology on Undergraduate Business Education Preparation Programs: A Model

ROGER RANKIN
Idaho State University, Pocatello, Idaho

The rapidly increasing development and utilization of technology in an ever-changing global environment demands major curricular changes in under-graduate business-teacher education programs in order to meet the needs of tomorrow's teachers. The Internet, local area networks, presentation software, multimedia, and more powerful hardware and software represent a part of the emerging technology in the world around us.

As professional educators, the more technology we encounter, the more we realize that it must be part of our curriculum. But how? The business-teacher education curriculum is already packed with skills courses, methods courses, courses for vocational certification, as well as economics, accounting, and business law.

When reviewing the typical business-teacher education undergraduate program, a dilemma appears. What is the best delivery system for this new technology-oriented curriculum? Can new technology be infused into current coursework and make it relevant? What would be included in a new course addressing advanced technology? With limited funding, how can a business-teacher education program access the latest hardware and software and stay up to date with the latest technologies?

This article proposes a model to help business teacher education programs keep up with the changing times and to help answer some of those vital questions. The undergraduate program, from which this model is based, is a 30-semester-credit-hour major in Business Education.

CURRICULUM DEVELOPMENT PROCESS

Software selection. "What" will be taught needs to be addressed first. This issue forces the business-teacher educator to make judgment calls. The model suggested here is based on the idea that "the teaching of concepts" allows for the most flexibility when trying to keep up with emerging technologies. The goal of preparing teachers with expertise in "all" the software they may encounter is not realistic. For example, this model does not recommend teaching as many word processing packages as possible. Generally, enough time is not available to do that, and it would mean excluding other content from the degree program.

To teach software concepts, the use of integrated applications programs is an option. Concepts of database, spreadsheet, word processing, and presentation applications can be taught with one software package, and the package allows for integration of applications. For example, one could take data from the database, transfer it to the spreadsheet, create a chart, and place it in a document created in word processing or make it a part of a presentation. Besides programs such as Microsoft Works, suite packages such as Lotus Suite and Microsoft Office are examples of tightly-integrated programs. These suite packages are also leading programs in the business world.

Word processing, spreadsheet, database, and computer presentation concepts may not change drastically in a short period of time. However, the software associated with these applications can change overnight. When selecting software, teacher educators should consider whether the software's user interface is widely accepted and is easy to learn and use. Today many programs use a graphical user interface with understandable icons. Some of the most popular programs in business use a combination of menus and icons rather than keyboard commands such as *Alt F9*. The software and teaching methodologies should maximize the transfer of "concepts" to new software and should shorten the learning curve.

Ways to keep up to date. Teacher educators must read current literature concerning expected changes in technology and study present trends in order to incorporate those into undergraduate programs. At the same time, teacher educators must be aware of current technology used in middle and secondary schools and in businesses. This requires that business teacher educators anticipate the needs of graduates, meet the needs of business, and make difficult predictions about technology—an almost impossible task!

Advisory committees. The first step in this model involves creation of an advisory committee of secondary teachers representing rural and urban schools with from one to five teacher departments and of business representatives. The teachers should be selected based on their expertise and current use of technology in the classrooms. Business representatives should be individuals involved in the hiring or supervising of secondary school business program graduates. The advisory committee should discuss the teaching of technology-related concepts versus specific software packages as well as future trends in technology.

After the advisory committee meeting, business teacher educators should design a developmental sequence of courses that provides a curriculum including everything from a cold-boot to using the Internet. The following model is presented as an example of such a curriculum. This model curriculum carries students through four courses utilizing a "build upon the foundation" philosophy that incorporates the following elements:

1. Objectives. A series of developmental performance-based objectives that sequence students' knowledge and mastery of technology.

2. Four courses. Three courses have technology integrated into the content, and the fourth course is related to advanced technology.

3. Four textbooks used throughout the curriculum. Each text is used in two or more of the four courses, allowing students to utilize their texts as their performance objectives demand increased mastery. Three textbooks are software specific and include beginning through advanced features. One is a generic book on technology.

4. Teacher and computer-assisted methodologies. These provide relevant teaching skills specifically related to the curricular content.

5. A portfolio system. Students build the portfolio through the sequence of courses. The portfolio includes activities and products the students create for future use in their classrooms.

By sequencing the performance objectives and utilizing texts in more than one course, students move from one course to another, gaining greater expertise. They learn advanced features of the software and improve their skills related to planning and delivery of technology-related instruction in the business education classrooms of tomorrow.

Students develop portfolios throughout the entire sequence of courses. The portfolios include everything from software-specific information of interest to them to formal assignments. The information is designed to be used in the real world of teaching by the student at a future time. Additionally, the students become confident in their ability to use technology.

LABORATORIES AND RESOURCES

Before making curricular changes, immediate issues to address are facilities and resources. Access to the latest software, hardware, and peripherals is needed so that students gain proficiency in the use of software and hardware.

A laboratory environment is perfect for delivery of the business education curriculum if it is configured correctly. Foresight in the technology arena is difficult, but time spent today considering expected changes in technology can allow for the best possible investments in equipment and software. Purchases of computer chips or CD-ROM drives that are predicted, by computer magazine reviewers, to be obsolete in a year would be unwise purchases even if they could be purchased at a great discount. Likewise, new releases of software and new hardware can have bugs that can cause teachers and students many headaches. While acquisition of the latest software is important, textbooks that teach the latest release of software may not be on the market for six months to a year.

Availability of technology/computer laboratories ranges from the optimal option of a fully accessible lab/classroom for business education undergraduate students to a situation where the lab must be shared with other departments or colleges. To improve accessibility to software, a portion of a file server in a networked computer lab can be allotted for course-specific software. In other instances, course-specific software can be installed on standalone microcomputers.

Computers with CD-ROM drives, fax machines, scanners, and printers are essential in order to give students valuable hands-on experiences and opportunities to create projects for their portfolios.

Other essential resources include textbooks and student template disks. Textbooks can contribute a great deal to the performance-based goals that span several courses. In this model the same textbooks are used in two or more of the courses in the sequence, providing for optimum use of the information and assignments.

Many times student template (data) disks accompany textbooks providing reinforcement of software skills. Using books and data disks with a consistent format improves the learning curve for students. By having students use the same texts in several courses in this performance-based curriculum, an organized, sequenced curriculum can be provided. The textbooks provide relevant and challenging exercises that match the increasingly difficult tasks in each class.

Software concepts can be taught using standalone programs such as Microsoft Word, WordPerfect, or Lotus 1-2-3 or by using an integrated program. When individual word processing programs are used, newer versions can be acquired at special "upgrade" prices.

Integrated software allows students to learn concepts of word processing, database, spreadsheet, and presentation applications. The software introduces the student to the power and convenience of an integrated software package. One form of integrated software is a suite package. A suite package may include a word processing, database, spreadsheet, and presentation program. When adopting a suite of software, hardware requirements must be taken into consideration. The new suites of software are impressive and powerful but require a significant amount of space. In order to stay current with technology, hardware upgrades may be needed to meet software requirements.

Microsoft Windows is included in the curriculum because of its current popularity and expected status in the future. Many labs run on MS-DOS, but make Windows and Windows application programs available. To run Windows 95 and new application programs designed to run under it, large amounts of RAM memory and hard disk space will be needed. With Windows 95 being a disk operating system, major changes in applications software are expected in the next few years.

A large number of software packages may be available in microcomputer laboratories throughout a university allowing students to achieve a working knowledge of them. This model curriculum encourages students to attend short workshops (i.e., one- to four-hour offerings) that relate to specific software, hardware, e-mail, local area networks, and university information systems provided by a central computer service center.

The following section describes the four courses in this model curriculum.

COURSE DESCRIPTIONS IN THE MODEL CURRICULUM

First course. The first course in the sequence allows students to learn the basics of the software utilized. For example, timed writings and production work introduce the student to word processing applications. Specific skillbuilding software, which can diagnose and prescribe keyboarding skills, is used to build speed and accuracy. As a result of this course, students become familiar with software-specific basics in word processing, and with software to improve speed and accuracy. This beginning course provides students with a taste of technology in business education. In this course various teaching methodologies are modeled and documents are produced for the student portfolios.

Second course. The second course introduces more advanced concepts of word processing, DOS, Microsoft Windows, the computer system, input devices, secondary storage, output devices, spreadsheets, database, graphics, and electronic communication. Word processing capabilities include macros, merging, columns, and tables. The same text and data disk used in the first course are used to support acquisition of new word processing skills.

Students are also introduced to integrated software during the second course. Microsoft Works, or any of the new suites of software, are very useful. Teachers may find it helpful to use the tutorial features that accompany software programs. They are excellent and provide beginners with online information and give them the opportunity to learn how to learn software. While working on applications, students should be encouraged to access tutorials that address specific features or problems that may arise. This approach shows students that they are never more than a few keystrokes away from relevant help. Students learn that the software is also a "teacher" in the classroom.

A "real life" integrated assignment can be a culminating activity. This assignment can be produced by the instructor to test the student's knowledge of integrated applications. The activity can involve having students prepare individual reports from the database, create a variety of charts from the spreadsheet, send form letters, and create labels. Students could produce documents in the word processing application that include reports and charts imported from the database and from spreadsheet applications. Effective use of fonts and styles can be required in reports and charts. Activities can include having students prepare and give presentations related to any aspect of this assignment.

Automated accounting is also included in the second course. Students are given secondary-level computerized accounting assignments so they become familiar with the software. In addition, members of business student organizations can be given sample tests in computerized accounting and be allowed to compete in postsecondary business student organization contests.

Beginning keyboarding software is introduced in the second course enabling students to see the effectiveness of teaching keyboarding on computers instead of typewriters. This introduces the concept of the changing role of the teacher as the facilitator in the learning process. Undergraduates become aware of the capabilities of the diagnostic and prescriptive aspects of the software. While using keyboarding software, students can take short and long timed writings, complete drills, and take the exit timed writing. This teaching methodology involves mixing skill building with production work.

Software related to teaching economic concepts is also introduced in this course. *The Jeans Factory* allows students to make decisions with respect to supply and demand, pricing, and hiring, or reducing a work force to make the most profit. *Up, Down, and Sideways* is a program that allows for student decision-making and then shows their decisions in relation to the entire economy. These programs require students to take many factors in our modern economy into consideration. Students learn that our economy is not a straight line and that peaks and valleys are normal.

A simulated exercise is required in the second course to provide the students with an overall view of the technology-related environment of the classroom. A budget of $50,000 is allotted each student, via a letter from a superintendent of a school district. The students are informed this money can be allocated to the business education program based upon an acceptable "microcomputer laboratory plan." Students are required to submit a proposal in an attractive format that addresses the following elements and questions:

1. Type, brands, and quantity of hardware and peripherals to be purchased. Justify your decisions based on current and future needs and justify the need for peripherals (i.e. scanner, laser printers, etc.).

2. Specific software requests and the courses in which they will be used.

3. Will the microcomputer laboratory be networked or have standalone work stations? Justify your decision.

4. Miscellaneous supplies that will be needed.

5. Include a detailed floor plan and identify essentials of a microcomputer laboratory.

6. Provide a detailed budget reflecting every item associated with the implementation of a new microcomputer laboratory.

The proposal must be substantial, complete, and thorough. Students must include this proposal in their portfolios. Upon entering the teaching profession, students will find this information to be very beneficial. Students learn and apply concepts of word processing, database, spreadsheets, and presentations by completing this proposal.

This course sets the stage for the third course in which the performance objectives require mastery of the software.

Third course. The third course in the sequence is provided so students can meet certification requirements in the area of office procedures/systems. Students gain proficiency in word processing and integrated software through numerous assignments. Several of the same texts are used in this course as in the others, allowing students to utilize the student data disks for reinforcement exercises.

The knowledge gained in the third course about word processing, for example, is applied in many assignments to insure that students can meet the performance objectives related to in-depth knowledge of the software. At the conclusion of this course, the majority of the functions of word processing and integrated software are mastered. More advanced technology is included in the final course.

Fourth course. This course emphasizes the use of technology in business education. Students should begin by becoming familiar with e-mail. Utilizing the Internet, students can contact other students in a number of colleges and universities around the nation as well as internationally. Working cooperatively with other teacher preparation programs, students can be required to send and receive messages, files, and fax documents as part of an "Internet Pen-Pal" activity.

Instructors should address students via e-mail almost daily. Course-related information can be communicated by e-mail, and evaluation (i.e. essay tests) can be conducted via e-mail. Teachers and students can send communications about student organizations, leadership conferences, and speakers on campus. Students should be encouraged to send messages to the instructor about problems encountered, ideas they have, and advisement needs. Through this series of activities, the amount of "paper documents" will be diminished.

Students can learn to utilize a fax machine in a number of ways. One of the more interesting activities is to have students create a macro in word processing. When the macro is activated, a fax cover sheet appears with spaces for all relevant fax information. Students fill in the necessary information and add the document to be faxed. Then students execute the fax.

In this course, students are introduced to local-area networks (LANS). They learn the functions of a file server, network operating system software, cabling, work stations, network adapter boards, and network application software. Students learn how each work station is able to access software.

Desktop publishing concepts are taught in this course and include the use of fonts, tables, line drawing, and graphics to create newsletters and brochures. Teacher educators must decide whether a specific desktop software program such as PageMaker should be taught or whether concepts of desktop publishing can be taught using one of the powerful word processing programs on the market such as Microsoft Word or WordPerfect.

In this fourth course, students learn to use a scanner and to save graphics and text files for use with a word processing program. They create a document containing both text and graphics and send the file to the instructor via e-mail. Once saved to a diskette and brought up as a word processing file, the file is printed and graded.

Electronic information systems unique to each campus can be introduced and students can learn how to access information related to weekly campus activities, the long-range weather forecast, or *USA Today*. They can look up information in a foreign university library via Gopher. Students learn how to work from their homes, via a modem, to find information from a user group or a bulletin board.

SUMMARY

With the limited amount of time in a business-teacher education curriculum, proficiency in a variety of software packages at the expense of learning a wide variety of other technologies is not wise. The emphasis on teaching software "concepts" and on specific methodologies that help students learn how to learn can improve transfer of learning for the rest of a student's life.

This four-course curricular sequence, teamed up with four textbooks, helps students achieve the performance objectives required and allows them to graduate having acquired basic to advanced technology concepts. By sequencing the performance objectives, students move from one class to another, gaining more information and improving their technology skills. Emphasis should be placed on hands-on teaching methodologies; however, in some situations, guest lectures and field trips are necessary. The development of student portfolios to be used in the real world of teaching provides students with a portfolio of teaching activities but, more importantly, a great deal of technological skill.

In this rapidly-changing technological world, business teacher educators will need to identify relevant performance objectives for students, acquire hardware and software that meets the needs of business and education, and utilize teaching methodologies that make it possible for students to learn how to learn new technologies in the future.

Part II

CHAPTER 4

Technology and the Development of Critical Thinking Skills

B. JUNE SCHMIDT
Virginia Polytechnic Institute and State University
Blacksburg, Virginia

MARGARET STIDHAM KIRBY
Virginia Department of Education
Richmond, Virginia

As the Information Age unfolds, the creation of information is accelerating. In this rapidly changing world, educators must ask how and what shall students learn? How will they access and utilize the flood of information? What teaching/learning strategies will best prepare students to function in a highly technical workplace? General agreement exists that higher-order or critical-thinking skills are required in our computer-driven society and that educators must respond to how these skills can best be taught to students.

In "This We Believe About the Future of Business Education," the Policies Commission for Business and Economic Education noted the need for business educators to emphasize critical-thinking, reasoning, problem-solving, and decision-making skills to prepare students for the 21st Century (Maxam, 1990). These higher-order skills are to be emphasized in addition to communication and technological skills. Integration of thinking and learning skills across the curriculum was the focus of a chapter in the the the 1989 Association for Curriculum Development yearbook (Ackerman and Perkins, 1989). In the chapter they discuss "when, how, and why might we cultivate such an approach to integration of thinking and learning skills."

The Secretary's Commission on Achieving Necessary Skills (SCANS) was established in 1990 by Elizabeth Dole, then Secretary of Labor. It included 31 members from the nation's schools, businesses, unions, and government (U.S. Department of Labor, 1992a). The Commission's work included determining the skills needed for successful employment, defining acceptable levels of skill proficiency, and suggesting ways to achieve this proficiency.

The Commission gathered information by visiting successful corporations, reviewing research, and, then, having a panel of experts compile a list of skills from those sources. Based on the information gathered, the Commission reported in *What Work Requires of Schools* (U.S. Department of Labor, 1991) that workers need five competencies and three foundation skills. The competencies included resources, interpersonal information, systems, and technology. In particular, interpersonal competency is the ability to work with others; while technology competency is the ability to work with a variety of technologies. The Commission also reported that three foundation skills are necessary for effective work: basic skills, thinking skills, and personal qualities. Basic skills include job-related technical reading, writing, mathematics, listening, and speaking skills. Thinking skills include creative thinking, decision making, problem solving, seeing things in the mind's eye, knowing how to learn, and reasoning. Personal qualities include responsibility, self-esteem, sociability, self-management, and integrity. Thus, critical-thinking skills evolved to a position of major importance in the SCANS efforts.

As a basis for recommending proficiency levels, the SCANS (U.S. Department of Labor, 1992b) interviewed approximately 100 individuals actually in the workforce. Represented were 25 high-wage and 25 low-wage jobs. Findings from the interviews supported the Commission's assumptions that individuals in high wage jobs display substantially greater proficiency in the competencies and foundation skills than individuals in low-wage jobs.

Thus, unanimous agreement among business and industry leaders, members of professional organizations, educators in general, and business educators in particular exists concerning the need to develop critical-thinking skills across the curriculum. However, how to accomplish the teaching of these skills while at the same time ensuring that students develop needed technological competence and basic academic skills must be addressed.

TEACHING TECHNOLOGY—PRESENT EMPHASES

Much of the present instruction that business educators provide for developing students' technology competence focuses on software specific step-by-step procedures. Essentially students learn "how to" but little of "why." They are not challenged to think beyond the use of specific software functions for producing a specific output. Further, all students in a class, generally, produce the same output. Following is an examination of four specific approaches that rely on these procedures: the "cookbook," the template, the "how to" video and audio tape, and the applications created from "scratch" approaches.

The "cookbook" approach. The teaching of spreadsheets involves the use of numerous formulas, which students usually enter following "cookbook" type directions. For example, students may be entering in a given spreadsheet cell the formula for calculating the percent of contribution that selling candy made to the total income of a retail specialty store. The formula is, of course,

$$\frac{\text{percent contribution}}{\text{of candy}} = \frac{\text{1995 candy revenue}}{\text{1995 total revenue}}$$

Using this approach, what the students learn about calculating the percent of contribution of candy to total revenue is shown here:

1. Move the cell pointer to D15
2. Type the formula +C10/C14
3. Press (Enter). the result, .24995, appears in cell D15.

Too often, the teacher assumes that the students know what the formula represents or that knowing what it represents is unimportant as long as the students push the correct keys. Further, they assume that students can interpret the result of .24995 as representing 25 percent. Unfortunately, the students gain little in terms of learning that can be applied and transferred to other situations. An opportunity to teach problem solving with application to the real-world use is missed.

As another example, look at the way students learn to sort on multiple fields in a database using this "cookbook" approach. The database is one for a nursery that keeps information about different types of plants sold.

1. Choose   Sort Records from the Select menu
2. Type   FLOWER NAME in the 1st Field box
3. Choose   Descend for the 1st Field
4. Type   DATE PLANTED in the 2nd Field box
5. Choose   Ascend
6. Choose   OK or press Enter

Obviously, the student who learns to sort from this information has little idea as to what is being done. The teacher must stand back and question just what the students are learning. Do they have a clear concept of what "descend" and "ascend" mean? Do they realize that the sort will first look for FLOWER NAME, beginning with flowers that start with "a." Then, as soon as flower names are sorted in descending order, a to z, the DATE PLANTED for each flower will be located, with output provided in ascending order if the same flower has more than one planting date. Again, students who learn how to follow only the "cookbook" directions learn very little that they can apply and transfer elsewhere.

The template approach. Software instructional materials, particularly spreadsheet software materials, may include templates that allow students to examine outcomes of various data input for a given situation or examine "what-if" outcomes. The templates provide a means for seeing the effect on outcomes of various input scenarios involving sales, purchases, investments, advertising, production, and so forth. Use of them can help in the development of thinking skills by comparing projected outcomes for various input data. Research undertaken by this author and a colleague (Schmidt & Gabris, 1993) revealed, however, that of 257 Virginia high school teachers responsible for providing spreadsheet instruction as part of the Business Computer Applications course, 28 percent did not teach "what-if" uses. Thus, even though business teachers have an ideal way to address the teaching of thinking skills along with the teaching of technology, they do not all seize the opportunity. Simply entering data in a given template without scrutiny of what the outcomes imply results in limited learning on the students' part.

"How to" video and audio tapes approach. A number of video and audio tapes to teach specific software are available. Use of these involves even more of a "cookbook" approach than instruction provided through the approach discussed previously. The authors, having personally learned several different software programs through the use of tapes, can testify to the extent of frustration users can experience. The learner becomes a "button pusher" with little insight as to functions and concepts being learned and why they are being learned. This mode of software technology instruction is further limited because the learner must be highly motivated.

Applications created from scratch. Some texts go beyond simply having students use prepared templates. They supply data and have the learner create the template, especially for data that lends itself to the use of spreadsheet software. Or data may be supplied for a database, with the learner being required to assign fields and create input screens.

These applications created from scratch set the stage for the development of higher-order thinking skills as the discussion in the last section of this chapter details. If students, however, learn only in the context of a specific application using specific software, their ability to transfer their learning to other situations will be limited.

Summary of current approaches to teaching software. In summary, current approaches rely heavily on students learning commands associated with specific applications and specific software. Most often, the teacher serves as the problem solver when the student "messes up" by not pushing the correct buttons. Little thought is given to helping students develop an understanding of the different functions the software performs nor of the meaning of the information they are entering. Present teaching emphasizes having students learn as quickly as possible to use the "power" or "bells and whistles" of specific software at the expense of understanding what they are learning and being able to apply that learning to other situations.

TEACHING TECHNOLOGY—EMPHASIZING SOFTWARE FUNCTIONS

To gain an understanding of the functions of software, students can be taught to visualize the use of software as detailed in the curriculum guide *Business Computer Software Curriculum Series, Part 1: Business Applications Software* (Virginia Department of Education, 1991). The nine functions of software with accompanying tasks at three levels—beginning, intermediate, and advanced—provided in the guide are:

- Vocabulary includes the identification of terms, concepts, and commands useful to computer operation and task performance.
- Access software tasks allow the student to get the software up and running.
- Data/text entry tasks are keyboarding operations and include entry of letters and numbers, and operation of special function keys.
- Editing tasks allow the student to add, delete, change, or reorganize data entered in the computer by key or mouse operation.
- Formatting tasks enable the student to arrange text or graphic elements on the page or in a document.
- Printing tasks are those related to printer access and operation.
- File management tasks help the student store and access information at the computer.
- Production includes assignments that apply a combination of tasks to realistic job activities.

- Troubleshooting tasks require the student to solve problems commonly encountered by computer users. (p. 3)

The guide cross-references the numerous tasks it contains by function and level of difficulty, as already noted. In addition, the tasks are cross-referenced by specific courses included in the business education curriculum and by seven software types including DOS, word processing, spreadsheet, database, graphics, data communication, and desktop publishing.

One of the major purposes for developing the guide was to help teachers get away from focusing on the teaching of specific software packages and, instead, to have students learn skills that will not become obsolete quickly.

Teaching tasks that are common across several software types helps students develop transferable technology skills. This approach also ensures that students are not locked into learning specific commands and producing output for specific software. Certainly, this approach will help students adapt in their future personal lives and careers as they encounter continually changing and updated software.

Emphasizing software functions does not ensure, however, that students are developing critical-thinking skills. In fact, most software-related instruction offered today, whether using the "button pushing" software specific approach or the teaching of software functions approach, provides few opportunities for students to learn to work cooperatively as members of teams. Even the software function approach allows the teacher to have all students doing the same thing at the same time, with little concern given to higher-order skill development.

TEACHING TECHNOLOGY—EMPHASIZING CRITICAL THINKING

If the approaches previously discussed do not involve students in developing higher-order thinking skills and do not address development of interpersonal qualities, then how can the teaching of software technology skills also incorporate these important skills? To help students build these skills, business teachers must be willing to take chances and not feel that all students must produce the same product to assure uniform grading. They must have students simultaneously working on a variety of different projects and activities involving the use of different data sets and different software packages. Obviously, the business teacher who teaches in this way will lose a degree of control. Students, on the other hand, will be challenged to take charge of their own learning.

Following are some examples of instructional strategies that can be used to help students develop higher-order thinking skills and the ability to work cooperatively with others as they use software technology skills. Before these strategies are used, students must be familiar with the software they are to use. However, teachers should not belabor learning the intricacies of the software before the strategies are used, as the students will gain in-depth knowledge of the software through these instructional strategies.

Example 1.
- STRATEGY: Students work in groups to solve software application problems.

- PROBLEM: Each student group of three to four students collects data that are to be represented graphically. The data can be collected through surveying class members, keeping track of stock market price changes for a period of time, taking inventory of types of computers in use in the school, and so on. Once data are collected, the group must determine how to best present the data graphically through available software.

- TIME TO COMPLETE: three to four hours in class for directions, checking on efforts to collect data, and preparing the graphics presentations.

- HIGHER-ORDER SKILLS DEVELOPED: Decision making, problem solving, reasoning, and teamwork.

Example 2.

- STRATEGY: Have students develop criteria for evaluating software.

- PROBLEM: Each student develops a set of criteria to evaluate word processing software. To help the students develop the criteria, have them use the nine functions outlined in the previous discussion as a framework for their criteria. As students develop the criteria, have them evaluate one another's work, providing one another with comments to strengthen their criteria. Students should be provided a checklist for completing their evaluations of one another's work. When students are satisfied with the criteria they have developed, they then use the criteria to prepare a word-processed instrument that can be used to evaluate word processing software. (Note: Using word processing software for this strategy is particularly effective as the students generally have a better knowledge base and thus more opinions as to what they like and dislike about it than other software.)

- TIME TO COMPLETE: three to four hours in class for directions, starting the projects, peer evaluations, and preparing evaluation instruments; three to four hours out of class for students to develop criteria and design formats for evaluation instruments.

- HIGHER ORDER SKILLS DEVELOPED: Decision making, evaluation, problem solving, and reasoning.

Example 3.

- STRATEGY: Using appropriate software, students create primary and secondary files that will be merged.

- PROBLEM: Using software with merge capability, have each student complete two files: a primary file and a secondary file. Have the students imagine that they are in charge of a Girl Scout troop, and it is their responsibility to coordinate a three-day camping trip. They must enlist the help of the parents of the 10 scouts in the troop who will be on the camping trip. The primary file will contain a letter explaining information about the trip—departure, arrival, activity schedule, location, and so on. Also, the letter will request that each scout's family donate something for the trip (something different for each family). The secondary file will contain names, addresses, and other variable information for the 10 families. Once the primary and secondary files are created, the students will merge the two files, entering variable information from their keyboards. Then, a second primary file needs to be created to print envelopes for the letters. This primary file is merged with the secondary file with the 10 family names.

- TIME TO COMPLETE: two to three hours in class to complete keying of letters, keying of names and addresses, and printing of merges; one to two hours out of class to develop letters and organize other information.

- HIGHER ORDER SKILLS DEVELOPED: Decision making, problem solving, and reasoning.

Example 4.

- STRATEGY: Interpreting outcomes for different financial statement input.

- PROBLEM: After students complete a computerized accounting simulation, have them examine what the statements might look like at the end of the next accounting period with different revenue and expense amounts. Have the students work in pairs to study current economic indicators and trends. These will then serve as the basis for their projections. (This strategy is particularly effective for helping students gain a comprehensive knowledge of the financial statements and what they mean.)

- TIME TO COMPLETE: two to three hours in class for the teacher to present the strategy and for the students to share and discuss projections of the different teams; two to three hours out of class for collecting information on current economic trends.

- HIGHER ORDER SKILLS DEVELOPED: Evaluation, decision making, problem solving, reasoning, and teamwork.

Example 5.

- STRATEGY: Have students work in teams of two to three students to prepare software manuals for different software packages.

- PROBLEM: The software manuals can be prepared for software the students have already learned as well as software they want to learn more about, such as CD-ROM software that may be available on only one or two computers. The teacher needs to provide general guidelines for the manuals. These guidelines should emphasize that the manuals are to be user friendly and should cover only main features of the software. Once developed, the manuals should be tested with members of other student teams in the class to be sure they are clear and complete. The manuals should include a title page, table of contents, application examples, screens or other displays as needed, and so on. The teacher must provide the students with criteria for judging the manuals prior to their beginning the assignment. For example, the criteria might be as follows: (1) Appearance, including formatting—25 points; (2) Accuracy of content—25 points; (3) Ease of use—25 points; Grammatical correctness, with 1 point deducted for each error up to the total for this criteria—15 points; Overall effort—10 points.

- TIME TO COMPLETE: five to six hours of in-class time; five to six hours out-of-class time. (Note: Some students will really become involved in this project and spend much more out of class time than the five to six hours.)

- HIGHER ORDER SKILLS DEVELOPED: Decision making, evaluation, problem solving, reasoning, and team work.

Example 6.

- STRATEGY. Have students, working as individuals, develop an application for a particular type of software being learned.

- PROBLEM: Assume that the students have spent several class periods learning to use database software. Then assign them to compile databases on their own and to complete queries and print reports from the databases. For example, note that the database must contain a minimum number of records, at least 15, each with so many fields of information, alphabetic as well as numeric. The reports must be ones useful for decision making and must be prepared according to given query directions. They should require that mathematical computations using information in the numeric fields be completed. Further, the students must prepare a written statement explaining the usefulness of their databases and the reports that have been prepared. No two students should create the same database. Here again, teachers must provide criteria for grading the databases, the reports, and the explanations of their usefulness.

- TIME TO COMPLETE: four to five hours in class for creating database formats, entering database information, and printing reports; four to five hours out of class for assembling database information, developing formatting details, and preparing explanations of usefulness of databases and reports.
- HIGHER-ORDER SKILLS DEVELOPED: Decision making, evaluation, problem solving, and reasoning.

The previous six examples just begin to explore the many ways that can be used to teach higher-order, critical-thinking skills while at the same time teaching software technology skills. These examples require teachers to assume responsibility for allowing students to be creative.

Using the strategies, a learning environment is created where students assume responsibility for their own learning. Thus, the stage is set for what students will have to do when they make the transition to the world of work —a world where they will be required to show that they can learn on their own, solve problems, make decisions, reason through diverse and complex situations, evaluate their own and others' work, and work in teams.

Using these strategies presents a challenge to teachers as well as students. Teachers must now be more creative in grading. No longer are all students completing the same exercises on the same software at the same time. Business teachers who accept responsibility for meeting the needs of today's students can no longer be satisfied with teaching only the "button pushing" aspects of specific software. They must explore ways to address the development of students' higher-order thinking skills while at the same time developing students' software technology skills.

REFERENCES

Ackerman, D., & Perkins, D. N. (1989). Integrating thinking and learning skills across the curriculum. In H. H. Jacobs Ed. *Interdisciplinary curriculum: Design and implementation.* Alexandria, VA: Association for Supervision and Curriculum Development.

Maxam, S. (1992). Teaching higher-order thinking skills: The need for research. *Business Education Forum.* 44:5, p. 31-39.

Schmidt, B. J., & Gabris, L. (1993). Emphases of spreadsheet instruction in high school business computer applications courses. Research paper presentation for Business Division, American Vocational Association, Nashville.

U.S. Department of Labor. (1992a). *Skills and tasks for jobs: A SCANS report for America 2000.* (Publication No. 1992-312-414). Washington, D.C.: U.S. Government Printing Office.

U.S. Department of Labor. (1992b). *Learning a living: A blueprint for high performance.* (Publication No. 1992-322-303). Washington, D.C.: U.S. Government Printing Office.

U.S. Department of Labor. (1991). *What work requires of schools: A SCANS report for American 2000.* Washington, D.C.: U.S. Government Printing Office.

Virginia Department of Education. (1991). *Business computer software curriculum series, Part 1: Business applications software.* Richmond: Vocational and Adult Education.

CHAPTER 5

Technical Training Methods

BRIDGET N. O'CONNOR

New York University, New York, New York

An instructor of microcomputer applications courses has a complex array of choices to make. First, the instructor must determine on which vendor's application packages to focus, which is an easy task when sufficient time and money are available. Next, a decision must be made regarding how students can best learn to use the application if teaching and learning resources are available. This is an easy task only when homogeneous classes exist, when the skill level, age level, and motivation to learn are the same for all students, and when time and money are unlimited.

The first decision—choosing a particular vendor's application package—is relatively risk-free because selection of any of the most popular applications is a good choice. Determining how students can best learn to use the package, however, involves experimentation and risk, as universal solutions seldom exist.

Universal solutions are rare because a methodology used in one environment is not always generalizable to other teaching/learning situations or even to the same classroom the next school year. In technical skills training, perhaps more so than in other academic arenas, instructors have varying knowledge bases, and students come with a wide range of ability levels. Universal solutions can hardly exist under these conditions.

Addressing the need to provide quality, consistent technical skills instruction may require changing the culture of some classrooms to allow for experimentation. Change is never easy; instructors hold dear their preferred teaching styles, and learners often expect traditional methods. Changing from a traditional teaching role such as knowledge disseminator to a coaching role and then back again is difficult for the teacher. If traditional teaching roles can change, traditional student roles can change also. In fact, students can and should play additional roles, such as peer consultant or tutor, allowing them to increase their knowledge and skill level.

Learning about learning is termed *meta-learning*. The construct of meta-learning means that instructors and students are able to experiment and learn from their experiences teaching and learning. Meta-learning means that instructors experiment with various teaching methods and learn which methods work. Meta-learning also means that students, likewise, play an active, directive role in choosing their learning activities and make choices based on their experiences.

Meta-learning for technical skills is creating an environment in which everyone—the instructors and the learners—are enmeshed in the technology. In such an environment, students learn under conditions similar to those in which they will be using their acquired skills. The actual application of technical skills requires that users be able to use learning resources, ask technical questions, and share their expertise with others.

In a classroom based on meta-learning, students observe their instructor learning new skills and sharing those skills with the class. Likewise, students share their newly found expertise with their peers. Meta-learning means that instructors practice what they preach. The instructor becomes a model, and learners see how they will be expected to keep their technical skills current. While role shifts may be uncomfortable at first, this process provides a model for lifelong, continuous learning.

Fortunately, a range of teaching and learning tools exists to support meta-learning. The purpose of this chapter is not to provide a comprehensive listing of methodologies to teach technical skills. Rather, its purpose is to provide an examination of tools that support learning in both student-directed and in teacher-directed approaches. This discussion also incorporates suggestions for creating a meta-learning environment.

LEARNING PRINCIPLES

The instructor offers students learning options based on the task to be learned, the learning style of the student, and resources available. In evaluating technical training tools and their effectiveness in the classroom, the instructor considers the following principles that are borrowed from pedagogy, andragogy (adult learning principles), behavioral science, and cognitive science. These are reinforcement, feedback, practice, and whole vs. part learning.

Reinforcement. When behavior is rewarded, it tends to be repeated. In fact, reinforcement that is part of a teaching/learning methodology serves to influence both learning and future performance. In finding a better way to teach, the instructor deviates from traditional methods and observes outcomes. Positive outcomes reinforce these shifts in teaching methods. However, applying any new teaching strategy involves taking risks. Experiments sometimes succeed and sometimes fail; but without taking risks, one never advances. In an environment that supports meta-learning, the potential of success outweighs the fear of failure. The reinforcement an instructor gets when a chosen method succeeds is the impetus to continue experimenting or perfecting the new method.

Reinforcement is important whether one is the instructor or the student. Instructors reinforce learning by offering encouragement and support. In addition, many technical learning tools have built-in reinforcement components. Proven mastery of one learning module, for example, encourages the student to progress to higher-order modules. Such a reward, or goal achievement, reinforces learning.

Feedback. Feedback, or knowledge of results, is also an important learning principle. How do instructors know if their students have done well or poorly if students' performance is not measured? Standards are difficult to establish in technical areas. However, one cannot teach if one does not assess. How can an instructor know if students have learned if the learning objective is unclear? Knowledge of results does not have to be equated with grades. Knowledge of results, however, does need to be correlated with desired learning outcomes.

Students obtain feedback from their instructors, their peers, and, increasingly, from their learning materials. Some software training tools are tireless coaches and evaluators. Moreover, this feedback can be individualized and can be prescriptive and evaluative. Knowledge of results is vital in pushing a learner from one skill level to another and serves as essential positive reinforcement.

Practice. Practice makes perfect. Practice sessions are needed for experimental sessions as well as for drill and practice sessions. Experimental practice sessions may mean the student is free to select what tasks may lead to the overall learning goal. Such sessions allow learners to focus on their individual needs, not those of their peers. Drill and practice sessions can have value where overlearning is the goal. For example, once startup procedures or frequent command sequences become automatic, one does not have to consciously think about them. This releases the learner to consider other issues related to the new task at hand. Practice supports learning retention and the transfer of learning by doing.

Whole vs. part learning. Behaviorists believe that knowledge is built on mastering a series of individual tasks and then assembling them to complete a larger task. Cognitivists believe, however, that while basic knowledge is very important, the learners can best learn to use and integrate parts by problem solving or seeing for themselves how pieces fit into the bigger picture. Instructors need to know the point at which a learner may be empowered to use learning materials effectively without an instructor's intervention.

Student- or self-directed learning is undoubtedly more a problem-solving exercise than a task-based exercise. Whole learning, akin to problem-based learning, means that students are forced to make connections by themselves, rather than have the instructor detail the connections for them. When learners practice at the application level, they learn not only more thoroughly but learn how to learn.

STUDENT-DIRECTED METHODS

When the student is empowered to learn how to learn, the instructor's role is to guide the process. This means that the instructor identifies, selects, and makes available appropriate resources and then guides or coaches students in the effective use of those resources. The role of the instructor is not diminished by the application of learner-directed methods. The role of the instructor changes from being a knowledge disseminator to being a facilitator of learning. Examples of student-directed learning include software manuals and tutorials, audio and video tapes, computer-based training, helpdesks, and online help. When using a helpdesk, a learner can telephone an expert for help with software applications at any time of the workday. With online help, a learner can get assistance through a computer network.

Software manuals and tutorials. A software manual can serve as a learning resource for the experienced user who needs to be prompted on how to perform a given function. To use this manual, which comes packaged with the software, a person needs to be relatively knowledgeable about the application.

If users are not familiar with that type of application program, the terms in the manual's index will be foreign to them, making it difficult to locate information. For advanced courses or advanced learners, user manuals can provide an excellent reference and source of information for self-directed problem solving.

Software manuals often include written tutorials on how to use the software. These tutorials can be useful in initial training efforts but are often difficult to follow for the first-time user. To overcome this limitation, a number of textbook and tradebook publishers have introduced easy-to-follow tutorial books. Some major software vendors, such as WordPerfect Corporation, are providing tutorial books and software manuals.

Audio and video tapes. Audio and video tapes add additional sensory communication channels to print-based learning materials. Audio provides an oral, human element to learning, while videotape provides an added dimension of visual instruction. Discussion, demonstrations, and examples assist the learning process. Typically, audio or video tapes are used in conjunction with print-based tutorials. A drawback to their use is that the user must manipulate the computer, the tutorial, and additional hardware—the video or audio tape player —at the same time. However, audio and video tapes allow learners to learn at their own pace and convenience.

Computer-based training. Computer-based learning materials consist of an alphabet soup of options, all using the computer as a training platform under the rubric of computer-based training (CBT): programmed instruction (PI) and computer-assisted instruction (CAI); computer-managed instruction (CMI); and interactive video (IV). Following is an overview of these tools.

Programmed Instruction (PI), as well as early computer-assisted instruction (CAI) are examples of linear instruction, meaning learners complete one lesson at a time, in a sequential, step-by-step manner. Programmed Instruction (PI) is often identified with the work of psychologist B. F. Skinner in the 1950s. Skinner designed a "teaching machine" that was based on the completion of small, sequentially advancing learning tasks to build toward advanced learning tasks. Skinner's "teaching machine" was later replaced by books called programmed texts. An early computer-based example of this concept was PLATO, a mainframe timesharing CAI system. PLATO offered extensive courseware because the expense of development was spread over a large number of users.

Newer CAI programs, however, allow microcomputer users to access learning modules in a multi-branching fashion. Random access better supports self-directed learning since the user can navigate among the learning modules, selecting topics of interest in whatever order is deemed logical. CAI systems are no longer limited to just text-based models. Today they include multimedia capabilities that integrate animation, video, and sound.

Computer-managed instruction (CMI) refers to the use of a computer to keep rosters, learner profiles, class schedules, and test scores. The merger of CAI and CMI has resulted in systems for testing, instructing, keeping student records, and prescribing and controlling individualized lessons. CMI systems can generate, administer, and score tests; many have built-in pre-and post-tests. With CMI, learners can determine their own mastery levels for given learning modules and decide when they are ready to demonstrate that mastery.

Interactive video (IV) is a multimedia learning system that combines the capabilities of video with CAI. It comes in four formats:

1. Interactive videotape
2. Laser disc
3. Compact-disc interactive (CD-I)
4. Compact disc read-only memory (CD-ROM).

Interactive video adds a visual and audio channel to traditional self-paced CAI systems. The computer provides the interactive feature that allows for self-paced and self-directed instruction. Because of the added sensory input of still pictures, video, and sound, interactive video can match many students' preferred learning styles.

To use the videotape format, the user responds to instructions on the video monitor. An interface device allows the computer to link with the video player, allowing the computer to match video with specific lessons. However, this process can be slow because a videotape does not offer random access. Interactive videotapes are the least expensive interactive video format. However, its use is expected to fade because it is complicated to use, specialized equipment is needed, and newer forms of media are available.

One newer form of media is the laser disc. The laser disc offers much higher resolution than videotapes and information can be accessed randomly. Large, single-purpose laser disc players are required that have one of three control levels:

- Level I has a standard VCR-type system that allows the user to control the instruction with either the player or the remote control.
- Level II has interactive branching software embedded in the disc and read by the player.
- Level III allows the laser disc player to be controlled by the computer.

The laser disc can provide high-quality stereo sound. Since there are two sound channels, they can be used individually to give the user a choice of a Spanish or English sound track, for example.

Phillips, the consumer electronic corporation, has attempted to develop a multimedia delivery standard known as compact disc-interactive (CD-I). CD-I is the term used for discs that can be played on an audio compact disc (CD) player, but that have additional interactivity features when the disks are played on the Phillips CD-I device. The CD-I device plays standard audio compact discs, game discs, and photo discs, as well as Phillips CD-I discs, and uses a television set as the display.

Compact disc—read only memory (CD-ROM) is considered the leading form of multimedia. CD-ROM overcomes the access limitations of videotape and is a relatively inexpensive multi-purpose type of equipment. Small, multi-purpose compact disc drives can be easily and inexpensively added to microcomputer systems. While CD-ROM is an excellent storage and retrieval medium for text, standard CD-ROM disc drives are very slow for interactive presentations that need immediate responses. As access time and transfer rates are improved, CD-ROM is expected to be the technology of choice.

To recap, computer-based training (CBT) options require that learners be participants in their learning experience. They must key in answers, touch the screen, or use a mouse to manipulate the system. Active learners comprehend more and retain more than passive learners. The use of CBT materials, therefore, should result in learners not only learning faster and better, but retaining the information longer.

Helpdesks and online help. Helpdesks and online help facilities are alternatives to face-to-face coaching. Most helpdesks (also called hotlines) offer centralized tutoring from a person at the other end of the telephone line. Online help is assistance from a computer-based source. Both services are highly interactive.

Helpdesks can be located within an organization, at the software vendor's site, or elsewhere over an 800-number. Helpdesk agents, trained in troubleshooting and personal relations, offer the learner immediate help. The objective of the helpdesk is to increase user satisfaction and morale by providing "just-in-time support." Highly trained helpdesk operators help perplexed users solve their computer problems.

Because of the flexibility of 800-numbers, vendors have a great deal of flexibility in assigning their help facilities. Digital Equipment Corporation's helpdesk, for example, is in Ireland, the site of a competent and inexpensive workforce.

Screen-sharing software allows a helpdesk assistant to view and manipulate the user's screen. This support greatly speeds up the "help" process, as users often have difficulty describing their specific problem. Using this screen-sharing software, the helpdesk operator can demonstration visually how to solve the specific problem. Because the demonstration is immediate and graphic, the value of the feedback is improved greatly. Screen-sharing software is built into many classroom LAN programs. Reminiscent of language-training labs, this capability allows the instructor to "tune in" to whatever the learner is doing.

One form of online help programs offers computer-based assistance, which is built directly into the software application package. Many programs offer context-specific help. For example, when a user has difficulty using the mail-merge function in a word processing program, the user presses the help key and is immediately shown printed instructions on the screen on how to use this function. Context-specific help is an increasingly important feature of nearly all best-selling software packages.

Another form of "help" is provided on CD-ROMs. A group of technical information specialists, Support on Site for Applications (SOS), for example, have compiled their secrets and troubleshooting tips on CD-ROM. This means that users can search for help on the CD-ROM just as if they were using a dial-up information service such as Dialog. Because instructors cannot be expected to know everything about a given application package, products such as SOS provide technical expertise at easy reach of the advanced learner as well as the instructor.

TEACHER-DIRECTED METHODS

Teacher-directed methods are most appropriate when the learner is a novice computer user or simply needs a lot of personal, face-to-face attention. Most teacher-directed methods are combinations of stand-up lecture and personal tutoring. Training aids that support teacher-directed classrooms are computer demonstration devices and generic software books.

Demonstrations. Instructors are often called on to demonstrate step-by-step procedures. Demonstrations may involve having the instructor use a single monitor to show a specific function to an individual student or a small group. In addition to the screen-sharing software available for use on networks, large group demonstrations can be aided by projection systems, such as LCD panels, LCD data/video projectors, CRT data/video projectors, and large video monitors.

LCD (liquid crystal display) panels can function as electronic transparencies or can be used to demonstrate software features, such as the creation of macros. The instructor can project computer images onto a screen that can be viewed by an entire class. These lightweight, portable devices, weighing about five to seven pounds, are used in conjunction with a high-intensity overhead projector (4,000-6,000 lumens). LCD panels come in monochrome or color models.

LCD data/video projectors, unlike the LCD panels described in the previous paragraph, offer high-level, graphics quality output and do not require the use of an overhead projector. However, projectors in this category are much more expensive than an LCD panel. These products are valuable when one needs to project high-quality output from a variety of media, including computer data, still or motion video from multiple sources, graphics, and/or animation.

CRT data/video projectors project RGB (red, green, blue) images similar to a computer monitor. Although these projectors produce a superior image, they are quite bulky and heavy. In practice, they are frequently mounted on a classroom ceiling.

Video monitors are simply very large video screens connected to the instructor's computer. One or several monitors can be located within a classroom to allow viewing by large numbers of students.

Well-orchestrated demonstrations can motivate the student to want to learn more. When the function is not too complex or too novel, a simple demonstration may suffice. However, simply showing a learner how a specific function works is not enough. Only by having the trainee repeat (practice) the procedure demonstrated can the instructor be sure that learning took place. Moreover, no matter how good the demonstration and the extent of practice is, learners are still likely to need to consult a manual or a help function from time to time.

Generic software books. Generic software books support conceptual learning of applications packages or provide applications exercises that are not limited to a single vendor's product. Examples are books that describe Computer Assisted Software Engineering (CASE) technologies, the principles of graphic design, object oriented programming, database design, and the like. These books can be used effectively when the objective of the course is not to do but to understand.

Generic software books are typically not recommended for the novice learner. However, when a concept is completely new, the instructor can use these generic books to motivate the learner to want to learn more. An example of a generic software is one that describes the Internet. In the case of the Internet, many people know it exists but do not understand how it operates or what its uses are.

The second category of generic books are exercise books. When a classroom has a variety of software options, or advanced students come with prior knowledge of a variety of spreadsheet programs, generic exercise books can assist the instructor who wants to pace students through exercises. When using these texts, the instructor (or the student) should have software manuals or other support materials available, as generic texts do not explain how to perform software-specific functions.

ADULT TRAINING METHODS

Adults seek out technical training for many reasons. Some want technical skills to master their current job, obtain a new job, or maintain professional certification. Many others, however, want technical skills for personal enrichment and for the joy of learning to use tools that will improve their self-esteem, communications, decision-making, or life-coping abilities. Much overlap exists among individuals in these categories. New York-based consultant Joel Levy says that learning to use software is seductive: The more one learns, the easier it is to learn, and the more one wants to learn! Following is a brief discussion of how business and academe are addressing issues related to supporting learners in their quest to learn more.

Adult training methods in business. Trainers in business settings use a variety of methods to ensure their workforce can use information technologies. Traditional classroom-based methods are widespread and popular but they involve the time and expense of having an instructor and students together in a room. Businesses are experimenting with a whole gamut of new training methods, attempting to discover the perfect match between organizational expectations and learner needs and abilities.

The term that best describes recent trends in adult technical training methods in business is performance support. Hartford-based systems specialist Elizabeth Regan defined performance support systems as technology that directly links training and support to performance (Regan, 1994). A performance support system might include online help and reference, hypertext, computer-based training, multimedia, and expert systems, as well as printed materials, video, classroom training, or other more traditional materials. Its objective is to provide information or assistance at the time the user needs it. Akin to coaching, performance support operates as a tireless teacher with an emphasis on quality. It is learner-directed, not teacher-directed. Following are a few examples of performance support concepts in action:

> J. C. Penney's performance support system of help, reference, and just-in-time training is integrated with their network of transaction processing systems that support their retail stores. Each of the 1,200 plus stores formerly relied on more than 100 reference manuals that had to be updated regularly. Online help and references were built into existing systems and all new applications include help and training capabilities built into the design. At J. C. Penney, hardcopy documentation is disappearing.

The objective of the Aetna Management Process (AMP) was to improve the rigor and quality of business analysis at Aetna. AMP is a set-by-step analytical process to assure that decision making never occurs in a vacuum, but is always undertaken with the company's mission and goals in mind. When it became apparent that conventional training was not accomplishing this objective, Aetna designed a PC-based performance-support tool to guide managers in executing the process, self-evaluating their own work, and creating appropriate deliverables.

Organizations often find that learner-directed education is an efficient, cost effective method. Furthermore, when it is tied into the concept of performance support, it puts the resources of the organization at the fingertips of the user. This just-in-time learning is considered the most effective type of learning.

Adult training methods in schools. Technical skills training should be a process of creating an environment in which students learn and practice life-long learning strategies. Instructors lead the learning process. Sometimes that means being directive; at other times it means ensuring that students have the resources to solve problems by themselves, as they will need to do outside the classroom. Like trainers in the business world, academics are experimenting with a wide range of methods to ensure that students have the technical skills they will need to be active members of the workplace and society.

While the establishment of performance standards is difficult in business, setting academic standards is even more complex. Most instructors have no direct control over the ability of students and little control over the learning resources that will be available. Many textbooks and learning resources are committee decisions, and this can impede the creativeness of a given instructor. Compounding this issue is the fact that instructors themselves come with a varying mix of skill levels. Some instructors have developed new innovative solutions. Following are examples from one university:

> The School of Continuing Education at New York University offers online applications instruction, called a "virtual classroom." In Richard Vigilante's virtual classroom, students at remote locations learn Lotus Notes at the same time that they learn to write Lotus Notes applications. Currently in its fourth year of operation, student feedback on the course has been excellent, and the school is working to expand its virtual concept to other information systems courses.

> Because of the wide range of cultural backgrounds, skill levels, and instructional needs of students in his classes, Professor Robert Burnham, professor at New York University, individualizes instruction. Self-directed learning materials are supported by instructor-led demonstrations of applications including geographic information systems applied to school district restructuring and group support systems applied to team decision making. The network itself offers most of the K-12 IBM educational software to prospective teachers and administrators.

CONCLUSIONS

As learning about learning occurs in technical classes, instructors are finding that skill-building techniques used previously are not appropriate for today's students and the often complex software applications packages they must master. Rote memorization of keyboard commands simply does not make sense when help functions and templates are readily available and when software is becoming so easy to use. Furthermore, keeping an entire class together stymies the growth of the fast learners and can pull an entire class down to the pace of its least capable members. Given the range of learning support tools on the market today and the heterogeneity of classes, instructors are experimenting with ways to facilitate learning.

The technical training tools described in this chapter—tutorial books, audio and video tapes, computer-based training, helpdesks, online help, projection systems, and generic software books—are used extensively in business and school environments. The concept of performance support, technology that directly links training and support to performance, includes the spectrum of these resources. The effective implementation of these tools, however, relies on several key elements.

One key element is that of fiscal resources; money is considered the universal decision maker because dollars are necessary to purchase materials. The choice of a software package does influence the type, quantity, and price of instructional materials. However, a lack of fiscal resources is often not the primary impediment to experimenting with new teaching/learning methods. Instructors must have the time and desire to learn to use new tools, and they must be willing to experiment with new instructional methods. The instructor must serve as a model and must help learners choose appropriate learning resources. In a meta-learning environment, computer knowledge and experience base is developed and is transferable to new operations for both the instructor and the student.

REFERENCES AND READINGS

Gosney, M., and Jerram, P. (1994). *Multimedia power tools.* New York: Random House.

Graves, P. R., and Kupsh, J. (1994). Computer-based and multimedia presentations. *Proceedings of the 13th Annual Office Systems Research Conference.* Springfield, Missouri: Office Systems Research Association.

Lewis, C. S., (1992). *Trainer's complete workbook for personal computer training.* Englewood Cliffs, New Jersey: Prentice Hall, Inc.

O'Connor, B. N.; Bronner, M.; and Delaney, C. (in process). *Training for organizations.* Cincinnati, Ohio: South-Western Publishing Co.

Regan, E. A. (1993). Integrated performance support (IPS): A new concept for a new era! *Proceedings of the 12th Annual Office Systems Research Conference.* Springfield, Missouri: Office Systems Research Association, pp. 1 - 10.

Regan, E. A., and O'Connor, B. N. (1994). *End-user information systems: perspectives for managers and information systems professionals.* New York: Macmillan Publishing Co.

Verducci, D. (1994, in press). The effects of three training methods on adults' attitudes and skills using microcomputers: An experimental study. *Proceedings of the 13th Annual Office Systems Research Conference.* Springfield, Missouri: Office Systems Research Association.

Weinberg, G. (1986). *Becoming a technical leader.* New York: Dorset House Publishing Company.

CHAPTER 6

Desktop Presentation Software—What Is It and How Can It Be Used?

PAT R. GRAVES

Eastern Illinois University, Charleston, Illinois

Desktop presentation software was first introduced in 1986, about two years after desktop publishing software entered the workplace. While today's desktop presentation software has some features of desktop publishing, it has its roots in both graphing and drawing programs. The term "desktop," as in "desktop" publishing, implies that developmental work is created on the desktop using a computer and related equipment. This type of software is also referred to as presentation graphics or, simply, presentation software. Its main purpose is for the development and display of presentation visuals. Visuals may also be referred to as slides, screens, or charts and can be displayed as overhead transparencies or viewed through computer-projection devices.

In its brief history, desktop presentation software has made remarkable advances in product enhancements and increased ease of use; concurrently, the programs have become significantly larger and require greater computing power to operate. For example, in the PC environment (as opposed to Macintosh), programs released during 1986-87 were DOS-based programs requiring 640K RAM space and 3-4 megabytes for hard disk installation. By 1991, these numbers had increased to 2 megabytes RAM space and 6-10 megabytes for hard disk installation.

WINDOWS-BASED PRESENTATION PROGRAMS

In 1993, products released were predominantly Windows-based and required 4 megabytes RAM space and 15+ megabytes for hard disk installation (in addition to the demands of Windows). The graphical user interface also has tremendously increased the need for faster processing speeds. While vendors may say that 386 processors will support these programs, performance is very sluggish and this contributes to user frustration when waiting for screens to redraw during development. In 1995, a complete installation may require more than 40 megabytes with 20 megabytes being the minimum space required. Because of these storage demands, vendors have begun providing programs on CD-ROM; a trend that is expected to continue in the future.

While many different programs can be used to develop visuals for presentations, the leading presentation programs today are:

- Lotus Freelance Graphics for Windows

- Software Publishing Harvard Graphics for Windows
- Microsoft PowerPoint for Windows and Macintosh
- WordPerfect Presentations for Windows or DOS
- Aldus Persuasion for Windows and Macintosh

Typically, these programs retail at $395-$500, but significant price reductions are available for educational institutions. Often a package is sold for a set price, such as $795, with permission to use it on 10 computers. Network versions are available, too.

DOS-BASED PRESENTATION PROGRAMS

DOS-based programs such as Bravo or Cricket Presents cost much less than the Windows programs described previously, but they have many of the typical presentation features. If history is a predictor of the future, cost reductions can be expected in the next few years.

If equipment and Windows software are unavailable to support these programs, Harvard Graphics 3.0 is an excellent and versatile DOS-based program and will run with 2 megabytes RAM space and 6.5 megabytes of hard disk space.

KEY FEATURES AND USES

The key features of desktop presentation software are:

- word processing capabilities
- drawing capabilities
- graphing abilities
- importing capabilities for clip art, photographs, or data from other programs
- exporting capabilities for transferring images to other programs
- screenshow development and display using text and diagram builds and, possibly, animation and digital video import
- presentation design and management
- printing capabilities.

Teachers will find desktop presentation software an invaluable tool for preparing visuals for their own classroom presentations; however, another aspect should be considered. These programs can be tremendous tools for teaching communication concepts. Principles of concise writing can be blended with techniques of color use, typography emphasis, and graphic enhancements for both visual- and print-based materials. Principles for accurately representing numeric information in graph form can be introduced. Students can learn to better organize their thoughts, assemble information, and create a computer-based screenshow to complement oral presentations. They might work collaboratively to develop these projects; and, if the technology is available, incorporate video and sound clips into their presentations to achieve elements of multimedia presentations.

Color, graphics, animation, and video are elements students find exciting and fun to work with on an independent and collaborative basis—and along the way, they will learn basic principles of communication. The features of desktop presentation software can help to motivate students; teachers have a responsibility to learn how to effectively use the programs to guide students' development.

This paper will provide more detailed information about desktop presentation software features, ideas for classroom use, and software and hardware considerations for development and projection.

DESKTOP PRESENTATION SOFTWARE FEATURES

While the user interface of these programs will vary, many of the same capabilities exist in each one. Features are selected using icons and drop down menus; screens are displayed in a WYSIWYG (what you see is what you get) style. Users may prefer one program rather than another based on perceived ease of use and specific features one program may have. Also, compatibility with other programs (for example, word processing and drawing programs) used becomes an issue if extensive file transfers are anticipated. However, standard features typical of all presentation programs are described in the next paragraphs.

Word processing capabilities. Text charts are usually the dominant chart type used in presentations. These charts convey text arranged as titles, text columns, and lists. Charts can be spellchecked individually or as a presentation group. An assortment of fonts are available in different styles and sizes. Text enhancements include justification and alignment options, line and letter spacing adjustments, drop shadows or other font treatments, and variable colors.

Drawing features. Graphic enhancements are incorporated into the design of presentation visuals with the drawing tools in desktop presentation software. While these will vary, most programs provide the following drawing tools: rectangle, circle, polygon, polyline, curve line, and freehand line. Solid and graduated (blended) colors can be applied to lines, circles, and/or boxes created with these tools.

Additional editing tools provide options for text and objects: rotating and skewing (slanting), grouping and ungrouping, connecting, deleting, copying, and front/back reverses. Extensive libraries of clip art (images and symbols) are provided with all programs; most programs provide a hard copy of these images with the appropriate filename for ease in using the visuals.

Graphing abilities. Graphs may also be called charts, and most presentation programs use the term interchangeably when referring to visual representation of numeric information. Chart galleries provide a quick way to select an appropriate chart type with a suitable appearance, and then edit it to replace existing data with new data.

Charts can be developed by filling in forms for the following types of charts: pie, bar, line, area, and scatter. Some programs have even more choices available. Variations in appearance can be achieved with 3D representation, color changes for backgrounds, and other chart elements.

For special effects, pie slices can be exploded (pulled out) or images (pictures) can be used in place of bars for pictorial charts. Because graphs convey general relationships between data sets, numbers can be displayed within the chart when precise data information is needed.

Numbers should be positioned to accompany slices, bars, or lines, or they should be placed in tables below or beside the visual representation. Users must learn how to select and adjust attributes effectively and to fill colors/patterns for text and other graph elements. Care must be taken to keep the graphs uncluttered and easy to understand.

Also important is careful use of

- legends—to describe shading or coloring used on the chart
- labels—to identify parts of the chart
- grids—to show scale and reference values
- tick marks—the coordinate marks on the grid that help with interpreting the chart values.

Organization charts can be used to display hierarchical information such as job titles in word form on connecting boxes. Color, fill patterns, and text treatment can be adjusted in an organization chart.

Importing capabilities. Importing involves bringing images or data into desktop presentation software from other programs. Although libraries of clip art and symbols are provided, additional clip art can be purchased on floppy disks or CD-ROMs. Often, these can be selected in categories such as business, education, presentation, holidays, etc. Graphic file formats must be compatible with the desktop presentation software and the artwork file to be imported.

Because of the large file size required for photographs, they can be purchased on CD-ROMs rather than diskettes. Also, original photographs can be scanned in black and white or color to create a digitized image for import and can be adjusted or fine-tuned with drawing tools. These images are brought in to the screen following the same simple procedure as retrieving a clip art image. However, graphic file formats must be compatible with the desktop presentation software.

Presentation programs can be linked to spreadsheets for direct transfer of numeric information into graphs using a feature known as OLE (object linking and embedding). As a spreadsheet is changed, the linked graph automatically adjusts. This is a tremendous productivity feature for people who use spreadsheets and graphs extensively. Some presentation programs can create text charts by importing text saved in an outline format with a word processing program.

Exporting capabilities. Complete charts or sections of charts representing text, graphs, or images can be exported into other programs. Several export graphic formats will be available with the software because the chart must be exported from the presentation program in a format that the program accepting the information can read. Logos, newsletter nameplates, or company letterheads can be created with a desktop presentation program. Then those images can be incorporated into word processing programs—programs that would not have the same type of drawing capabilities. Graphs can be created and imported into word processing programs to be used in reports.

Screenshow development and display. Besides automating the process of presenting a series of charts, a screenshow can be used for file organization. By creating a screenshow, a table of contents is created that lists all files related to one topic. This listing has several important advantages:

- The presentation list displays only the file names of the charts for the current topic and not all files on a disk; this is beneficial for file retrieval and sequencing.
- The series of charts can be spellchecked instead of checking each chart independently.
- The same background, font treatment, and color characteristics can be applied to the entire series by using presentation appearance settings.
- The entire series of charts can be printed as a presentation instead of independently; charts can be printed in full size or in miniature form for speaker notes, handouts, or file copies.

Another purpose of a screenshow is to automate the process of presenting a series of charts, sometimes called pages or slides in a presentation. A presentation can be viewed on a single computer, or, with projection equipment, projected in black and white or full color for large screen viewing by an audience. It can be free running or the pace can be controlled by the presenter. A free running presentation shows (in a timed sequence) all charts in a specified order. For example, a screenshow can be set up to change pages in the presentation every 15 seconds.

When the presenter controls the pace, the presenter touches the spacebar or clicks a mouse button or a remote control device. Being able to pause during a presentation is especially helpful when additional explanation or audience interaction is expected.

Screenshows are typically displayed in a linear fashion with each page appearing in the same sequence from the beginning of the list to the end of the list. However, some programs provide a "hypershow" capability by incorporating "buttons" to control a branching or looping function. The buttons act as "go to" statements so that when the presenter clicks on a button with the mouse, the presentation will "go to" a certain chart in the series. Several buttons may be used in one presentation.

Presentations can be easily edited or rearranged, or pages can be removed from the presentation. One can add special effects—how the pages make their entrances, how long they remain, and how they exit from the display. Although many different transition effects (fade or dissolve, open, wipe, overlay, etc.) are available, a presenter should limit the variety used in one presentation. Too many different on-screen movements may seem confusing to the audience. Two possible transition techniques are:

- Use the same transition for all charts pertaining to the first topic—then a different transition for the charts pertaining to the second topic, etc.
- Use the same transition throughout the presentation with a different one used for title charts as each topic is introduced. These charts serve as helpful dividers for the audience.

Transition features are actually a form of animation. One might think of animation in terms of Saturday morning cartoons or Disney movies. While current desktop presentation capabilities for making objects move on the screen are not that sophisticated, even a little animation can be very compelling for business presentations. For example, a title could fade or drop into its location and text arranged as a bullet list could appear as a "build series" with one line appearing at a time.

Using transition capabilities, business models could be displayed by building and connecting the model parts as the verbal explanation progresses. For special effects, clip art can be animated; for example, an arrow could hit a target or a stop light could blink off and on. The possibilities are unlimited.

Video and sound can be used with presentation software, also. While some clips may be available with the programs, users would probably want to obtain additional libraries on CD-ROM. Here is where the line between desktop presentation software and multimedia software begins to blur; and as presentation software becomes more sophisticated, the line will become even less distinct. This increase in sophistication of desktop presentation programs is analogous to the blending of word processing and desktop publishing programs.

Presentation design and management. Several presentation design and management techniques were discussed related to screenshow capabilities. A consistent presentation appearance can be achieved by using a pre-designed "slide master" which controls the background, text treatments, and color characteristics in all pages in a screenshow or series. To create a presentation, a user would:

1. Select a predesigned "slide master."
2. Select the type of page layout—title, bulleted list, chart, artwork, or a combination.
3. Type text, create a chart or artwork, or add clip art.
4. Add a new page or slide.
5. Repeat Steps 3 and 4 to complete the presentation.
6. Save the presentation.

This process is very quick and efficient with professional-looking results. Programs provide "slide sorting" by displaying multiple pages of a presentation on the screen at one time. Their sequence can be rearranged by using the mouse to drag a page to a new location and dropping it into place.

Most programs provide some form of "clipboard" capability for copying text or other objects from one page and pasting them into other pages. Context-sensitive help is available to provide assistance related to all features of the programs.

Runtime capability. A "runtime" feature is important when a presenter is using projection equipment and a computer without presentation software. This feature allows the presenter to save a complete screenshow on a 3½-inch disk and then take the disk to any computer connected to a projection system and display the screenshow without using presentation software. To advance from page to page in the screenshow, the presenter would press the computer spacebar. This feature can be used for linear sequencing of pages but not for hypershow presentations.

Output capabilities. Presentation output can be created in several ways. A screenshow is a form of output. Slides can be created by using a film recorder to create the screen image on 35mm film, which is then developed as slides.

If enough use justifies it, a school or business could have its own film recorder; if not, files can be sent on disk or by modem to companies called "service bureaus" for development.

Virtually any printer ranging from a $200 dot matrix to a $12,000 color laser can be used with presentation software to prepare handouts or presentation transparencies. Even at the lowest end, an effective transparency can be created by printing a black and white visual on a dot-matrix printer. And then taking the printout to a copy machine to make the transparency. With a heavier acetate transparency material, black on clear transparencies can be produced by ink jet or laser printing directly on the transparencies.

Be careful that the transparencies used for laser printing or photocopying are designed for the appropriate type of equipment. Thermal transparencies used with laser printers could cause considerable damage to the printer because thermal transparencies are not made to withstand the necessary heat used to produce the image on a laser printer. Special laser printer transparencies must be used in laser printers.

Of course, color output is more interesting than black and white—but more expensive. Color printers use different technologies such as ink jet, thermal transfer, or laser; the costs of this equipment vary widely. Color will increase in popularity as the costs for both equipment and supplies continue to drop and competition for improved document appearance fuels market demand. However, at this time, color laser printers are the most expensive printers. Even at the lower prices, color printers can be used in schools for special design projects such as flyers, brochures, and presentation transparencies.

After designing colorful images on screen, students will naturally want to create colorful printed output; therefore, a teacher can capitalize on this higher motivation level to develop students' creativity and teach them design considerations regarding effective use of color for visual- and print-based materials.

CLASSROOM APPLICATIONS

Presentation software can help teachers prepare better visuals for classroom purposes—regardless of the output method selected. This output choice will depend on the available equipment, time available for development, and appropriateness for a given situation. Teachers will be willing to devote more developmental time to a teaching unit or module if it can be used again in the future; if it is a one-time application, then a simple transparency may be the best media choice.

Even a series of black-on-clear transparencies can be designed with readable fonts and a consistent look achieved through simple graphic enhancements. The use of color greatly expands the design possibilities. While color adds the potential for unlimited variety, color should not be used randomly. Color is an important communication tool to add emphasis, code related items, or indicate levels of importance.

Using screenshows provides many advantages in the classroom:

- Convenience—Because the screenshow is saved on a disk and projected from the computer with projection equipment, nothing else is needed for the presentation. This eliminates aligning transparencies or covering a transparency to display only part of it at a time. One disk holding all files is less costly than 10 or more transparencies.

- Flexibility—Images can be changed or adjusted immediately before a presentation or even during a presentation. Speakers might want to incorporate an element of interactivity so the class/audience could have a voice in how the information is presented.

- Professional image—Since changing the projected visuals is so easy, the speaker can concentrate on presenting ideas and promoting discussion. Speaker knowledge of subject matter will be apparent to the audience, too, because he or she will be so familiar with the material developed as visuals. These subtle behavioral differences serve as cues, making the speaker seem more professional and more credible.

- Motivation—Students find taking notes easier when well-designed visuals help guide discussion. As mentioned earlier, using color, graphics, animation, and video can make class presentations more interesting and fun for the students. Often they will be more willing to listen to the ideas being presented.

First, a teacher should learn to use presentation software effectively and then provide instruction for students on how to use it. Presentation projects (individual or collaborative) can be incorporated into many different classes through the preparation of screenshows and print-based materials. Students could learn to prepare various graphs, export them in a graphic format suitable for their word processing program, then import them into reports and other documents they are creating.

Even outside the classroom, opportunities exist. Promotional materials could be developed for student organizations using the desktop publishing capabilities of presentation software to prepare flyers, brochures, and letterheads. Screenshows could be developed for department or school promotions at open houses, fairs, or any other event where the public could be informed about programs within a school system.

SOFTWARE/HARDWARE CONSIDERATIONS

As mentioned at the beginning of this article, as presentation software increases in sophistication, the hardware requirements also increase. A product comparison appearing in *Presentations Magazine* (Tuck and Frankel, February 1994) reviews the features of 31 presentation programs for DOS, Windows, OS/2 and Macintosh systems. Listed prices range from $79-$695.

Preston Gralla (September 1993) provided the following table in an article reporting an evaluation of the five leading Windows presentation programs by *PC/Computing* staff. Four of the five programs earned *PC/Computing's* "seal of approval." Reviewers ranked Freelance Graphics 2.0 very high in ease of use and rated it the best presentation package—it was the product of choice for rush jobs and team presentations. WordPerfect Presentations 2.0 was noted for sound effects; however, Harvard Graphics 2.0 was selected for being the ultimate in sound and light shows. Aldus Persuasion 2.1 was not rated as high as the other programs. In the table, ✓ indicates the software has a particular feature; ✗ indicates it does not.

	Lotus Freelance Graphics 2.0	Software Publishing Harvard Graphics 2.0	Aldus Persuasion 2.1	Microsoft PowerPoint3.0	WordPerfect Presentation 2.0
Phone	(800) 343-5414	(800) 336-8360	(800) 333-2538	(800) 426-9400	(800) 451-5151
FEATURES					
Price	$495	$495	$495	$495	$495
Disk space required (minimum/full)	8MB/18MB	8MB/21MB	2MB/10MB	5MB/14MB	4MB/20MB
No. of master styles	65	31	7	160	64
No. of chart styles	108	88	83	1	192
OUTLINER					
Drag-and-drop slide moving	✓	✓	✓	✓	✓
Collapse and expand levels of text on slides	✓	✓	✓	✗	✗
Set charts in outliner	✓	✓	✓	✗	✓
DATA IMPORT					
1-2-3 for Windows	✓	✓	✓	✗	✓
1-2-3 for DOS	✓	✓	✓	✓	✗
Excel	✓	✓	✓	✓	✓
Quattro Pro	✗	✗	✓	✗	✓
DBF	✓	✗	✓	✗	✗
Preview graphics	✓	✗	✗	✗	✓
No. of clip-art images	552	536	100	573	1,010
SCREENSHOWS					
Directly play sound and video	✓	✓	✗	✓	✓
Launch programs from screenshow	✓	✓	✗	✗	✗
SUMMARY					
Pros	Easy to use; packed with presentation power.	Deepest charting capabilities best screenshows.	Good outliner.	Excellent import capabilities and special effects.	Simple to use; excellent graphic manipulation.
Cons	Multimedia could be beefed up.	Not the easiest to use.	Hardest of the programs to use.	Charting features could use help.	Poor chart editing.
Verdict	Best of the bunch for everything except multimedia.	For industrial-strength charting, screenshows, and multimedia.	Wait until the next version.	Useful for those who work with imported graphics.	Best for using sound in presentations.

Since this table was published, version 4.0 of Microsoft's PowerPoint was released with significant improvements. In one review, Ed Bott (February 1994) indicated that a complete installation required 42 megabytes of hard disk space, a considerable increase from version 3.0. In another review, Richard Jantz (December 1993) indicated a price of $395 for Harvard Graphics 2.0 for Windows.

Another program that could be used for presentations is Corel Draw. Although it began as an illustration program, many presentation features have been added. Other presentation programs, Micrografx Charisma, Gold Disk Astound for Windows, and Asymetrix Compel, are designed to incorporate elements of multimedia. These programs are very memory intensive with libraries of photo images, sound effects, music clips, and video clips.

Projection equipment. To take advantage of the many benefits computer-based screenshows provide, projection equipment connected to a computer is necessary. Although the costs continue to drop, full-color projection is still expensive. Here are the available options with some of the advantages and disadvantages of each.

- LCD (liquid crystal display) panel—These lightweight devices lie on top of an overhead projector and use the light emitted by the projector to create the image displayed on a large screen for audience viewing. Older projectors adequate for transparencies are not bright enough for use with LCD panels; a high-intensity projector (4,000 to 6,000) lumens is required. Monochrome LCD panels are available, but the color panels are far superior for presentations purposes.

  While these two pieces of equipment allow dual use of the projector (for transparencies or screenshows), switching equipment by removing the LCD panel during a presentation is rather cumbersome. Some LCD panels are quite slender and designed for easy transport while traveling to different presentation locations.

- LCD data/video projectors—These units use a similar color creation technology as the LCD panel, but they contain their own light source and do not require the use of an overhead projector. They are portable and suitable for still or animated images and for video that is projected on a large screen for viewing.

- CRT data/video projectors—Using cathode ray tube technology similar to a computer monitor with RGB (red, green, blue) color, these units provide superior image quality. Units are often mounted on the ceiling because the units are large. The computer image is projected on a large screen for viewing.

- Video monitors—Monitors similar to televisions provide another alternative. Units are available in many sizes and can be permanently mounted in a recessed area of a wall or suspended from a ceiling. For greater flexibility for presentation locations, some units are designed as movable units on wheels. No separate screen for audience viewing is required since the images are viewed from the monitor screen.

Of these four options, only the video monitor could be viewed effectively with standard room lighting using present-day technology. To achieve color clarity essential for readability, the overall lighting in presentation rooms (teaching, meeting, or training rooms) must be reduced. Ideally, rooms should have a dimming capability, allowing the illumination level to be raised or lowered as activities in the room change. Variable lighting is needed so the viewing area can be made darker than the audience seating area.

Many vendors produce projection equipment; some of them produce more than one type. A few of the leading vendors are nView, Barco, NEC, Mitsubishi, Sharp, and Proxima.

Additional hardware options. Although not required, a scanning device would permit the inclusion of paper-based images by scanning them in black and white or in color. This process digitizes the image, which can then be saved in one of many file formats appropriate for different presentation programs. Scanners are available in hand-held or flat-bed models. A high resolution will produce the best image.

While screenshows can be prepared with images appearing in a timed sequence, usually speakers want to control when the next image will appear. Because this requires pressing a key or clicking with a mouse, the speaker must move close to the computer used for projection. To make this easier, remote control devices permit a speaker to advance the images in a screenshow from anywhere in the room. Pen-size laser pointers can be used by a speaker to call attention to something by shining a light on the large screen image.

Additional software options. After learning to use the fonts and clipart that accompany presentation software, users may want to add additional software to their collection for use with presentation software. Fonts and special font treatments such as textures, patterns, and depth can be achieved with programs such as Qualitype, Typestry for Windows, Pixar One Twenty Eight, or EZ Effects. A few of the clip art programs are Presentation Task Force, Click Art Incredible, Images With Impact, and Masterclips, Inc. Many programs are available only on CD-ROM because of file size requirements.

To transfer graphic files from one format into another, HiJaak Pro or Freeze Frame for Windows are good programs to use. The ability to capture any screen image is another capability of those programs that would be very helpful for teachers writing software instructions.

For presentations incorporating animation, video, or sound, many new programs and libraries are being released on CD-ROM.

CONCLUSION

Presentation software use holds many benefits for teachers, students, and anyone required to stand in front of a group and share ideas. Presentation charts can help to convey ideas in ways words alone cannot—especially when displayed with computer-projection equipment. When these charts are prepared by the presenter, that individual will be more organized because of the development process required to prepare the charts. By going through the creation and development process, the presenter's ability to convey the information effectively is increased as well as the presenter's confidence.

Presentation software is an important tool for more effective communication—users of this software have a responsibility to master techniques for designing quality visuals to enhance the communication process. Regardless of the type of output selected for these visuals—transparency, slides, or screenshows—the message is still of primary importance. The visuals will not replace the speaker; instead, they will help the audience understand the speaker's ideas.

REFERENCES

Becker, D. (February 1994). The big pitch: Sales presentations. *Presentations Magazine,* 8:2.

Bott, E. (February 1994). Bring down the house with Microsoft's PowerPoint 4.0. *PC/Computing,* 7:2.

Braun, E. (June 1993). Visual presentation tools sharpen communication style. *The Office,* 117:6.

Gralla, P. (September 1993). Presentation power. *PC/Computing,* 6:9.

Graves, P. R. and J. Kupsh. (March 1994). Computer-based and multimedia presentations, *Proceedings of the Office Systems Association Research Conference.*

Jantz, R. (December 1993). Harvard Graphics 2.0 for Windows and WordPerfect Presentations 2.0 for Windows. *Publish,* 8:12.

Kupsh, J. and P. R. Graves. (1993). *How to create high-impact business presentations.* Lincolnwood, IL: NTC Publishing.

Lindstrom, R. (February 1994). Showing off: Putting your best foot forward is good business and good for your career. *Office Systems 94,* 11:2.

Meilach, D. Z. (June 1993). Visually speaking. *Presentations Magazine,* 7:6.

Pearson, L. (June 1993). The medium speaks. *Presentations Magazine,* 7:6.

Rabb, M. Y. (1993). *The presentation design book—Projecting a good image with your desktop computer.* Second edition. Chapel Hill, NC: Ventana Press.

Strickland, T. J., Jr. and R. E. Shiffler. (September/October 1993). Computer projection panels: Technology for the classroom of the 1990s. *Journal of Education for Business,* 69:1.

Tuck, L. and D. Frankel. (February 1994). Presentation software offers power and flexibility. *Presentations Magazine,* 8:2.

CHAPTER 7

Multimedia: An Educational Tool

HEIDI R. PERREAULT

Southwest Missouri State University
Springfield, Missouri

The question to ask regarding multimedia is not if it belongs in business education, but how business educators can make the best use of the options and flexibility multimedia technology offers. Multimedia is not a solution to any specific educational problem; it is a means for creating instructional materials and for providing students with opportunities for learning and personal expression.

The challenge facing educators is determining how to best incorporate multimedia lessons into an existing learning environment. This article examines how business educators can use multimedia technology as a teaching and learning tool. The following sections provide an overview of multimedia technology, a rationale for incorporating the technology, and a review of multimedia hardware and software requirements.

OVERVIEW OF TECHNOLOGY

Multimedia technology is a tool appropriate for all levels of education. It provides the mechanism for integrating a variety of medias into the curriculum and for providing an interactive learning environment where students can advance at their own pace.

Multimedia presentation capabilities. Multimedia presentations combine all or some of the following elements: text, still images, full-motion video, sound, animation, and computer graphics. The presentation itself is available to one or more people through a computer.

The power of multimedia is not the variety of components, but the delivery. During a multimedia presentation, the audience is able to interact with the presentation. The interaction is most often accomplished through a computer keyboard, touch screen, or mouse. This ability to move the student from a passive receiver to an active participant is what provides the important difference between a multimedia presentation and a presentation using multiple media, such as film clips, textbooks, and tape recordings.

Allowing the user to control the pace, to branch to specific areas of interest, and to respond to cues or questions imbedded in the presentation gives control of the learning process to the student. Multimedia technology allows students to examine different aspects or situations relating to a selected topic. For example, although the entire class may be studying small business management, multimedia allows one student to watch a video segment providing a broad overview of managing a small business while another student, who is more familiar with the topic, elects to examine proposed legislation requiring small businesses to provide health-care benefits to workers.

Multimedia provides students the flexibility to investigate areas of interest or to review topics as needed. Students become more responsible for their own learning by making judgments on their own progress and selecting areas to investigate in depth. Although a one-on-one approach to education is available through the technology, students are not isolated from one another. They are in the same classroom studying the same broad topic. The increased flexibility multimedia offers students and teachers is one of the reasons educational institutions are willing to make major investments in the technology.

Multimedia success stories. The following examples are from schools that have incorporated the technology into existing programs. Although in some cases the technology is limited to certain academic areas, the most impressive successes are those school systems that have embraced multimedia as a teaching/learning tool across the curriculum. As a teaching/learning tool, schools must always have acquisition of knowledge foremost in mind; otherwise they can be lulled into the belief that multimedia's "bells and whistles" are more important than teaching cognitive knowledge in the fields of English, history, science, math, and business.

One school that has made a significant commitment to multimedia technology is the Exeter-West Greenwich Junior/Senior High School in Rhode Island. The goal is to have multimedia used across the curriculum. Faculty are hired with the expectation that technology will be part of their teaching methodology. Each teacher has a computer and every student has easy access to a computer. Not only is multimedia used as a delivery tool for lessons, multimedia is also used by students as a means to present their findings. Students are encouraged to express themselves using multimedia technology.

The philosophy at Exeter-West Greenwich is that seeing the technology is not sufficient; students must learn to use the technology. Their administrators and faculty believe their students are showing more creativity and teamwork as they utilize the technology and that students recognize technology as a tool to be used to accomplish tasks ("Multimedia for Everyone," 1993).

The Cuyahoga Valley Vocational School in Ohio is another example of a school that encourages both teachers and students to use the technology to present information. The resulting excitement about learning is so obvious the administration receives telephone calls from parents wanting to know what is going on in the classroom. Parents report that for the first time their children are actively sharing what they are learning in school.

The enthusiasm for learning is especially important to the instructors at Cuyahoga Valley teaching in the "at risk" program. The teachers see a change in attitude regarding coming to class and to education in general. The director of the Cuyahoga Technology Center is quick to point out that the technology is not the focal point of the instruction, but the means for providing options to students to support and enhance the learning process ("IBM Multimedia," 1994). The amount of time spent learning the technology should be weighed against the actual cognitive learning that occurs.

Other schools have a specific area in which multimedia is used. The University of Illinois uses multimedia to teach chemistry. The interactive video-discs contain lessons and laboratory demonstrations. One obvious advantage is that students do not have to be in a lab to conduct an experiment. Other less obvious advantages are that hazardous materials are not actually handled and students can advance at their own pace without having to wait for an instructor to be present. After completing the lessons through multimedia, the student is ready to advance to a wet lab. Instructors report that students are better prepared when they do enter the lab and have a more positive attitude toward chemistry ("The Acid Test," 1991).

The Patchogue-Medford School District, Patchogue, New York, found an innovative approach to literature. Traditionally, all students had the same homework assignment. They were to read specific chapters and be ready to discuss those chapters the following day in class. Now students select a chapter and become the expert on that section of the novel. Their specific task is to create a multimedia presentation demonstrating their understanding of the symbolism evident in their chapter(s). The result is a creative presentation that not only shows their grasp of the literature, but also requires students to use interpersonal, problem-solving, and organizational skills. The teachers at the Patchogue-Medford School District see increased student motivation and are extremely pleased with the resulting teamwork and creativity exhibited by the students (McDermott and Combs, 1991).

Many more success stories could be added. These examples show multimedia being used at various grade levels and that multimedia is not subject specific. Ideally, the technology will be shared across the curriculum and not limited to one subject area. Therefore, the first step toward incorporating multimedia is determining if the school system is ready to make a commitment to obtain the necessary technology and to provide training to educators and staff members.

RATIONALE FOR MULTIMEDIA

Not all educators are convinced that multimedia is worth the expense of purchasing the technology and the time required to learn a system well enough to create quality multimedia presentations. Some are concerned that multimedia presentations are little more than attempts to amuse students. These critics see the technology as the "dog and pony show" of the 1990s. They have a point. Just as a film can enhance learning, it also can be used to fill up an hour.

Before an investment is made in the technology, educators and administrators within a school system need to state the educational goals the technology will help them achieve. Teachers must then determine the level of commitment they are willing to make to learn how to create multimedia presentations themselves and how to incorporate the technology into their teaching.

Set goals. As school districts consider making an investment in multimedia technology, a logical first step is to state desired goals. Some realistic benefits likely to be achieved through the use of multimedia technology are presented as guides for setting those goals.

Reduce learning time. A multimedia presentation takes advantage of multiple stimuli. Students hear, see, and interact with the presentation. For a traditional, teacher-directed lesson, learning time includes the original presentation plus any re-teaching time for students who did not comprehend the material during the class presentation. What can be difficult to factor in is the time wasted by those students who were capable of moving on to more challenging material, but who were held back by those students in the class who needed more instructional time.

Multimedia presentations allow students to move on when they are ready. Although the studies regarding learning time through multimedia instruction are limited, they do show that students learn the material faster when multimedia is used as an instructional medium. One study examined the IBM Principle of the Alphabet Literacy Systems (PALS), an interactive video-based course. The findings showed "increases of more than two years in reading and writing skills with only 100 hours of instruction" ("Doubling Retention," 1993).

Mastering subject matter. A multimedia presentation has limitless patience. The student can interrupt to ask questions or can review material over and over again as needed and never feel embarrassed. Built-in check points are not grades, but are a means for evaluating whether a student should advance or review a section. Students are encouraged to experiment and can explore areas of personal interest without feeling others are bored or making judgments about them. Multimedia presentations also provide students with ready access to research materials. The student does not have to move to another location (library) to search for materials, but can simply "click" on an icon for related information.

Multimedia-based lessons provide all the advantages of individualized learning with the additional enhancement of student interaction. Students find the material more interesting than traditional text-based individualized modules, and they are provided with more opportunities to explore areas of interest.

Computer-based instruction has been shown to increase student achievement by about 30 percent, according to the 1992 "Report on the Effectiveness of Technology in Schools" ("Report on," 1992). A slightly more conservative figure is reported by the National Education Corporation, revealing a "25 percent improvement in retention with interactive video courses" ("Doubling Retention," 1993).

Provide access. For many school districts, it may be impossible to provide teachers to cover all the subject areas students wish to study or to provide opportunities for students to attend cultural events. Multimedia provides that access. Through interactive simulations students can have access to expensive laboratory equipment, or they can travel to foreign countries, or they can tour famous art galleries. The technology provides students with experiences that would otherwise not be available.

Multimedia also offers students the opportunity to study potentially dangerous subjects, such as electronics or chemistry, without risking injury. Multimedia allows students to experience the consequences of touching the wrong area or mixing the wrong substances without exposing themselves or others to danger.

Use technology. Information is a valuable commodity for all careers. To prepare students for the workplace, it is important to go beyond teaching them about technology. Students need opportunities to use technology to locate and to share information. Multimedia allows students to get hands-on experience using technology to obtain information, and it allows them to use technology to express themselves.

Although learning to create high-quality multimedia presentations could be a full semester course, in most cases it will be taught in conjunction with other software packages. If multimedia presentations are incorporated across the curriculum, students will need basic instruction on how to use the software and peripherals early in their educational experience. Their expertise will be increased as they use the software in various courses.

The expectations of teachers will increase as students advance to higher grade levels. Each instructor will be responsible for providing examples and suggestions pertinent to the assigned task for that specific course. Ideally, students will view multimedia as a communication tool and will not associate it with a specific discipline or course.

Because of their computer application and communications expertise, business educators can take a leadership role in providing multimedia instruction and support to students, teachers, and staff.

Provide training. Time is required to learn to use multimedia technology. If instructors will be using multimedia technology as a tool to deliver instruction, two options are available. The instructor can purchase commercially-prepared multimedia presentations or the instructor can produce custom-made presentations. If prepared multimedia presentations will be purchased, teachers will need to be able to set up and operate the multimedia equipment. This may include CD-ROM, laserdisc players, and projection devices. Minimal instructional time will be required for educators to learn to operate the equipment. Two or three in-service meetings will suffice.

Educators who plan to create their own or who plan to have their students create multimedia presentations will require a much longer learning period. The educator must learn how to create a presentation with a specific software package; this means learning a development system that is similar to a programming language. Educators must also learn how to operate peripherals, such as scanners, CD-ROMs, laserdiscs, microphones, and projection devices. Additionally, some instruction in design and layout will be needed to ensure the presentations are visually appealing.

Production time includes all the hours spent developing a presentation. This may include recording sound clips, videotaping speakers, and creating graphics, as well as linking the related sections into a professional presentation. An important point regarding production time, however, is that all multimedia presentations will not be full-blown productions. Multimedia presentations can include short segments to help students grasp the difficult aspects of a lesson, to provide variety, or to insert current event items into related textbook-based lessons. A one-hour presentation can take from 30-200 hours to produce, depending on the quality desired.

Business educators may find they need less learning time than most educators because they are used to learning new software packages and may have design and layout background from their exposure to desktop publishing concepts. Several resources are available to educators who want to learn more about multimedia. The following resource list has several useful books, periodicals, and catalogs.

RESOURCES

Periodicals

New Media
HyperMedia Communications
415-573-5170
$48/year (12 issues)
Free to qualified subscribers

T.H.E. Journal
714-730-3739 Fax
Free to qualified subscribers

Electronic Education
Scholastic Inc
212-505-4900
$23.95/year (8 issues)
Free to qualified subscribers

Multimedia Review
Meckler Corporation
203-226-6967
$35/year (4 issues)

Multimedia Today
Redgate Communications
800-779-2062
$19.95/year (4 issues)

Multimedia Solutions
800-426-9402 X170
Free

Multimedia World
PC World Communications
415-243-0500
Free with PC World
$19.97/year (10 issues)

Books

Interactive Multimedia
Ambron & Kristina
Microsoft Press

Managing Interactive Video/Work
Multimedia Presentations
Robert Bergman & Thomas Moore
Educational Technology Pub.

Desktop Multimedia Bible
Jeff Burger
Addison-Wesley Publishing

Macintosh Desktop Presentations
Sueann Hooper, eds
Steven Anzovin
Computer Publications

Multimedia: Making it Work
Vaughn Tay
Osborn/McGraw-Hill

Creating Multimedia on Your PC
T. Badgett & C. Sandler
John Wiley & Sons

Catalogs for multimedia products

Multimedia Solutions Courseware Catalog
Dept ZVO
1133 Westchester Ave
White Plains NY 10604

Agency for Instructional Technology
Box A
Bloomington IN 47402-0120

Triangle Technology
CD-ROM Titles
1441 Branding Lane
Downers Grove IL 60515

Quanta Press
1313 Fifth St SE
Ste 223A
Minneapolis MN 55414

ITC
13515 Dulles Technology Dr
Herndon VA 22071

McGraw Hill
11 W 19th Str
New York NY 10011

Compton NewMedia Inc
2320 Camino Vida Roble
Carlsbad CA 92009

Allegro New Media
387 Passaic Ave
Fairfield NJ 07004

Maryland Interactive Technologies
PO Box 1054
Reisterstown MD 21136

Wilson Learning Corp
7500 Flying Cloud Dr
Eden Prairie MN 55344

Time Warner Interactive Group
2210 W Olive Ave
Burbank CA 91506

Shipley Associates
PO Box 460
Bountiful UT 84011

Creative Multimedia Corp
514 NW 11th Ave Ste 203
Portland OR 97209

Info-Disc Corp
4 Professional Dr Ste 134
Gaithersburg MD 20879

MULTIMEDIA SOFTWARE

If students will be using the software to create presentations, the software selection decision is very important. Some programs and their accompanying documentation are much easier to use than others. If students will be expected to create presentations with limited instructional time, the software must be user-friendly and require very limited or no programming experience.

Software includes the basic authoring package, which provides the backbone of the presentation and other software packages used to enhance the presentation, such as a graphics package. All authoring packages have some basic features. Each allows the author to select and then link or branch text with video, audio, animation, or graphics. When evaluating multimedia authoring packages, consider the computer expertise of those who will be using the package and the professional quality desired for the presentations.

Four popular packages will be compared in the next section. The packages are Linkway Live!, Hypercard, Multimedia Toolbook, and Authorware Professional. As with all software, in the future these programs may have more features, be easier to use, and be less expensive.

Linkway Live! Linkway Live! by EduQuest is a relatively low-cost MS-DOS product. A network version is also available, making it attractive to schools wanting to provide multimedia to students in a lab setting. Linkway Live! has an easy-to-follow tutorial and has been used successfully by students in elementary schools to create short presentations. Students use the mouse to make selections. Students create "folders" complete with pictures, original art work (created with the paint program), text, and buttons. The buttons provide the user with options. A user can "click" on a button for more information or to return to another page.

Overall, the product has considerable appeal for getting students quickly involved in creating multimedia presentations and for allowing young students to use technology. The advanced multimedia user will want more options than are available through Linkway Live!.

Hypercard. Apple users have been using Hypercard to create multimedia presentations since 1987. The user creates "stacks" of "cards" to produce a presentation. A card is a single display of text and graphics. Sound and animation can be attached to the cards. The cards are linked to others in a stack with buttons to create a presentation. Upgrades in the product have increased its capabilities and made the program easier to master. Drawbacks to the program include the limited support for color and the lack of control over external devices, such as a videodisc player.

Hypercard is a good choice if students will be using the technology to create presentations. Apple provides Hypercard with every Macintosh sold, making it an economical choice for Mac users.

Multimedia Toolbook. Multimedia Toolbook, a Windows-based product, is an extension of Asymetrix Corporation's earlier version called Toolbook. Multimedia Toolbook is a powerful program designed to take full advantage of CD-ROMs, sound, video, and animation. The learning time is longer than the time required to learn other comparable products because of the coding needed to create even simple applications. A person willing to devote time to learn Multimedia Toolbook will be able to create impressive presentations.

Multimedia Toolbook, version 1.53, is a relatively low-cost product, but the product would not be appropriate for young students.

Authorware Professional. Macromedia's Authorware Professional was developed with education in mind. It has the ability to handle multiple-choice questions and to respond to incorrect answers. The developer can specify that the viewer not be allowed to advance until an acceptable score is obtained. The student (viewer) can be automatically cycled back for a review of the material.

Creating a presentation is accomplished through "drag and drop" icons and dialog boxes. The learning time for Authorware Professional is much less than products requiring coding such as Multimedia Toolbook. Another feature that will appeal to those wanting to have students create multimedia productions is the ability to "glue" sequences together. One student can work on one segment of a presentation while another creates a second segment. The segments can be "glued" together into a seamless presentation.

The advantages of the product are the relatively short time required to learn to create a basic presentation and the interactivity it allows the author to incorporate into the presentation. Authorware Professional is available in both a Windows and Macintosh version. The main drawback to Authorware Professional is the higher cost, approximately $1,000 for schools, which is more than three times the cost of some other programs on the market.

HARDWARE REQUIREMENTS FOR MULTIMEDIA

Once the decision is made to incorporate multimedia into the curriculum, educational institutions must then decide how to use it and to what extent it will be used. The decision will dictate how many multimedia computer workstations are required. If students will be using the technology to create multimedia presentations, labs with both production and playback stations are needed. If multimedia will be used only as a delivery tool, playback stations for individualized learning situations are needed and video display capabilities are needed in classrooms where presentations will be shown to entire classes. Once the intended use is decided, hardware decisions can begin.

Platforms. The first decision is which platform your school will support. The three most popular multimedia platforms for education are Apple's Macintosh, Microsoft's MPC (DOS compatible), and IBM's OS/2-based Ultimedia. It is wise to select a single platform to avoid the expense of incompatibility and duplication.

The platform selection decision should be based on the hardware already available to the school, local vendor support, and the preference of the staff using the computers. More off-the-shelf multimedia packages are available for the Apple and MPC platforms, so they are currently the two platforms most often used in educational settings. Once Windows/95 reaches the marketplace, newer and easier to use multimedia programs may be developed to run on that platform.

Specific hardware needs will depend on the intended usage. Playback stations require fewer peripherals than do production stations. Whether the hardware is for playback, production, or both, it is best to plan ahead and select equipment that has the capability for you to add new features or extensions.

Playback stations. One of the key needs for a multimedia playback station is lots of memory and adequate processing speed. Suggested minimums for memory are 4MB (megabytes) of RAM and 30MB hard disk. The minimum standards of a 386SX-class IBM-compatible or a 68020-based color Macintosh may not meet ones needed in the very near future. The rule of thumb when purchasing is to get as much memory and processing speed as your budget allows. To view video, some people predict that 32MB of RAM may be needed in the future to provide resolution similar to television quality.

Viewing. Viewing a multimedia presentation requires a quality color monitor. For group presentations, a large screen monitor or projection device is necessary. Three viewing options are provided for large group presentations:

1. Large monitors (37 inches or more) provide quality display. A 37-inch screen, however, is too small for a large classroom. Larger monitors provide better visibility for classroom presentations, but add the problem of limited mobility and higher cost.

2. Video projectors offer excellent quality for large classroom presentations. The projectors, however, are 80 to 100 pounds, so mobility is a problem. Some of these projectors are built into the ceiling. High-quality color projectors are very expensive, although costs are coming down.

3. A popular choice for classroom presentations is a Liquid Crystal Display (LCD) device. LCD panels are lightweight (9 pounds) and are used with overhead projectors. The quality is not as sharp as a video projector or monitor, but the newer models use active-matrix technology that allows full-motion video to be displayed. The April 1993 issue of *Electronic Learning* presents a buyer's guide comparing the cost and features of 11 LCD panels.

Storage. Multimedia presentations require considerable storage capacity. CD-ROM and laserdisc technologies are popular choices for multimedia storage.

Many off-the-shelf multimedia presentations are available on CD-ROM. Because of its ability to deliver presentations that need considerable memory capacity, such as those containing full-motion video clips and lengthy stereo audio segments, CD-ROM technology is experiencing wide acceptance. To play back a presentation stored on CD-ROM, a CD-ROM drive is needed. Macintoshes have built-in CD-ROM drives, as do many PC compatibles. To compare the features and prices of CD-ROM drives, see the 1993 Multimedia Tool Guide issue of *New Media*.

Laserdiscs are becoming a common storage medium for multimedia presentations. Popular multimedia authoring packages have laserdisc control facilities built into the program. These features simplify the process of accessing video or sound clips from a laserdisc. The user can simply click on a button to activate the video clip or stereo-quality soundtrack. The fast access time eliminates the "wait" often experienced with multimedia presentations that must access a video clip from other storage mediums. To use a laserdisc, a laserdisc player is needed.

Sound. Sound is an important feature of multimedia presentations. Although many computers have built-in speakers, you may want to purchase quality speakers so you can take advantage of the sound quality available through the multimedia presentations. The cost for speakers ranges from very inexpensive to hundreds of dollars. The investment decision should be made based on the quality of sound required and the size of the audience. (The April 1993 issue of *New Media* lists the features and prices for popular speakers used with multimedia.) If presentations are to be viewed/heard by individual students in a lab setting, earphones are the best choice.

Production stations. Production stations allow the user to create multimedia presentations. The equipment required for a playback station (except the large audience display devices) are the same as those needed for a production station. Additional peripherals are required.

Sound. To add sound to a multimedia presentation, you can either capture or record sound. Most CD-ROM drives can play standard music CDs. With the help of multimedia authoring software, you can select the music or sounds you want from a CD and incorporate (capture) the sound into your presentation. If you want to bring into your presentation "live" sounds, such as your narration, you will need a microphone and a sound card to record your sounds. Some computers, like the Macintosh, have built-in audio capabilities, but most will require a sound (audio) card to capture or record sound.

Visuals. Visual images are a major component of multimedia presentations. Full-motion visuals, graphics, still photos, and animation allow the author to create visually appealing presentations. To capture visuals, several options are available. If the author wants to incorporate original video into the presentation, a camcorder is used. A scanner or digital camera will allow the author to input still pictures. CD-ROMs and laserdiscs are popular sources for video.

To bring a video clip into a presentation, a video-capture board is required. The most pressing technical problem is the amount of memory required to store even the smallest video segments. To reduce the memory requirements to workable levels, expensive hardware-based compression products are required. Newer products on the market are worth investigating. Apple's Quick-

Time and Microsoft's VfW (Videos for Windows) allow for video input with only the addition of a digitizer (board). This provides quality video at a lower cost. Another more recent innovation is a combination audio and video card.

SUMMARY

Multimedia technology is a tool for all educators. It is not the answer to all educational problems nor is it necessarily appropriate for all settings. The technology provides educators the opportunity to enrich courses and to provide students with educational options that they otherwise would not have the opportunity to experience.

The first steps in adopting the technology are to set realistic goals and to provide training to those who will be using the technology. The decision regarding which multimedia authoring program to purchase will depend on the amount of computer expertise (including programming) those who will be interacting with the software already possess. If students will be using the software to create presentations, the software needs to be very user friendly. The desired quality of the presentations will influence purchase decisions. Some of the lower cost programs are easy to learn, but do not offer the options or the quality that the higher-priced packages provide.

The challenge presented to educators is to make judgments regarding how to best utilize the available technology. Business education teachers are likely to be early adopters of the technology because of their computer expertise; however, the technology is not subject-matter specific. The biggest gains to a school district may be obtained when the technology is adopted across the curriculum and when students are involved from a young age with creating multimedia presentations.

REFERENCES

Multimedia for everyone. (November/December 1993). *Multimedia Solutions* 3(6): 19-24.

IBM multimedia energizes "at risk" students. (1994). *Multimedia Today* 2(1): 33-35.

The acid test: Five years of multimedia chemistry. (September/October 1991). *Multimedia Solutions* 5(5): 50-52.

McDermott, V. and Combs, E. (September/October 1991). Breaking the cycle: Multimedia motivates high I.Q. underachievers. *Multimedia Solutions* 5(5): 40-42.

Doubling retention. (March/April 1993). *Multimedia Solutions* 3(2): 7-8.

Report on the effectiveness of technology in schools. (1992). *Software Publishers Association*.

Electronic Mail, Bulletin Board Systems, Conferences: Connections for the Electronic Teaching/Learning Age

MARIE E. FLATLEY

San Diego State University, San Diego, California

JENNIFER HUNTER

Western Carolina University, Cullowhee, North Carolina

We're surrounded. Whether today's new technology is referred to as a super-highway, global village, or the infobahn, it represents the notion of connectedness. Bill Gates has been espousing his "Information at Your Fingertips" theme since 1990 and is continuing to integrate the concept into new products and new versions of Microsoft programs. For example, Windows 95 software now contains tools to access the Internet (Rodriguez, 1994) as well as tools to access multiple mail sources (van Kirk, 1994).

Ross Perot, Al Gore, and other national politicians have been promising open access to information superhighways, and general business publications have been praising businesses that use technology for competitive advantage. Today we live in an age when technology is becoming more supportive of our intellectually intensive tasks.

Three of these technologies; electronic mail, bulletin boards, and electronic conferences; have become standard ways for gathering, sharing, and distributing information in businesses. With electronic mail (e-mail), a sender transmits memos or other documents over a computer network to either a single receiver or multiple receivers. The physical limits of location are no longer an issue. Messages sent are usually considered private.

Bulletin boards, on the other hand, provide a public place on a computer for senders to post messages or information and for receivers to gather information and comment on it.

Conferences are real-time meetings that are online. They give people the ability to talk with others in different places and with people who have different levels of interest and expertise. All of these technologies are experiencing rapid growth in the numbers of people using them.

This chapter describes these technologies as well as some ways to use them in the classroom. It also touches on the media most frequently used with e-mail, bulletin boards, and local and wide area network conferences, commercial services, and the Internet. At the end of this chapter, a list of references for further reading is presented as well a list of vendors for some of the products and services discussed in this chapter.

In writing about this new electronic age, one might use the analogy of the opening of the electronic frontier as being similar to the impact the railroad had in opening up the West or to the discovery of electricity or the invention of the automobile. In any case it is an exciting new territory that will capture students' interest and give instructors one of the most powerful teaching tools ever.

UNDERSTANDING CONNECTED TECHNOLOGIES

E-mail, bulletin boards, and conferences can be truly empowering technologies. Knowing ways to connect to those technologies is important. With a computer, a modem, and the proper software, connection to these networked systems from nearly anywhere on earth is possible.

Media types. While wireless connections using radio waves will become popular in the future, at this time the predominant media used to connect electronically with others include local area networks (LAN), commercial services such as CompuServe and Prodigy, and the Internet. Some cities or special interest groups have set up their own independent systems to serve their citizens or members; however, only the most widely used forms of media are discussed here.

LANs. When computers are linked to a network file server within a building or relatively close geographic area, it is on a local area network (LAN). The file server is a computer on a LAN that stores network software, applications software, and user files.

One can send e-mail, use bulletin boards, and talk electronically with anyone on a local area network provided the software for these applications is running on or accessible to the file server. In most cases, people who use networks can also share peripherals such as printers, storage devices, and CD-ROMs. One doesn't need to know how a network functions to use it to gather, share, and distribute information; however, one can get more from it by knowing some of its features.

While some companies believe in keeping their LANs closed to outside connections for security, many LANs are linked to other LANs or have gateways to other computers at remote sites. When LANs that are geographically dispersed are linked together, they are referred to as wide area networks (WANs).

Two different types of hardware are used to connect a LAN to other LANs or other computer systems. Similar LANs can be linked using a device called a bridge. With a gateway device, dissimilar LANs can be linked together and LANs can be linked to mainframe computers. A gateway translates protocols between dissimilar networks.

Both bridges and gateways allow information to be sent from one network to another in such a way that both networks or computer systems communicate as though a single network existed. Once hardware is linked properly to other computers, the platform being used (Macintosh, UNIX, or DOS-based) will be unimportant to the user.

Commercial services. Another medium to use for connections is a commercial service. These services provide a wide variety of services including e-mail, bulletin boards, and computer conferences.

Some of the most popular public subscription services are CompuServe,

Prodigy, America Online, GEnie, and Delphi. To use these services, generally a modem and communications software are needed. In fact, most of these services have communications software designed to help navigate their services easily. Many commercial services can be used simply by pointing and clicking. The software can be set up to dial the access number, insert the user name and password, and bring up a pre-selected screen.

These services have different and constantly changing pricing structures, structures designed to fit the needs of various users. To subscribe, one can order by phone via 800 numbers or purchase the software at local computer hardware or software stores. Sometimes the software is bundled with new computers or modems, but one still must sign up for the service. New accounts are usually allocated a few hours of free time to get acquainted with the service.

Here are what the menu screens look like for Prodigy and CompuServe. Notice the intuitive interfaces and the point and click format. In most commercial programs, the screen color and content can be modified to serve the user best. See the envelope in the lower right hand corner of the Prodigy screen; it tells the user there is e-mail waiting. With a sound system, a voice will let the user know "You have new mail." The CompuServe screen uses icons and drop down menus to navigate the service. It, too, has a voice feature welcoming the user to the service.

Figure 1—Prodigy Opening Screen

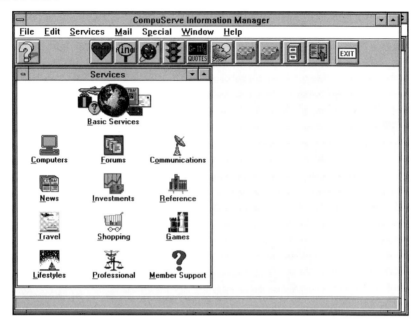

Figure 2—Compuserve Sign-on Screen

The Internet. The Internet is currently the largest network of linked computers in the world. These linked computers use a common method of transferring data and a common addressing system that transfers information from one computer to the next without going through a central computer.

The Internet began as a Department of Defense project and expanded to include education and other governmental agencies. Recently, it has expanded to include commercial, nonprofit and private organizations. The number of users is growing rapidly, numbering thirty million or more (Angell and Heslop, 1994). The Internet is unique in that it is run by volunteers and most costs are borne by users, who buy their own computers and provide their own connections. Like the other media described, Internet provides users with e-mail, bulletin boards, and conferences, which are called discussion groups or echoes on the Internet.

Another unique feature is that the Internet has no central administration; therefore, until recently, locating information using Internet was difficult. However, to help users find their way around Internet, four software search tools are available—Archie, Veronica, World Wide Web (WWW), and Wide Area Information Systems (WAIS).

Archie is a search tool used to help examine Internet archives worldwide by filename. It tells the user where a particular file can be found. Veronica, on the other hand, searches a collection of menus usually organized by subject called gopherspace. World Wide Web is a newly developed hypertext tool used to browse through resources in bulletin boards (Usenet sites), files for distribution (FTP sites), and subject files (Gopher sites). Wide Area Information

Systems (WAIS) is a search tool that searches database indexes by keyword on the Internet. These tools are some of the most helpful ones available at this time.

Some software used to access the Internet is more user-friendly than those described previously. Subscribers to private access services often get software that enables them to point and click rather than enter archaic commands such as ftp ftp.eff.org.

A program garnering attention today is Mosaic, a free navigation tool that runs under the World Wide Web hypertext tool (Tetzelli, 1994). Another free program is Cello. Some of these programs have a bookmark feature, allowing users to mark places so they can find their way back to them easily. See in Figure 3 how the easy-to-use bookmark feature in Cello is accessed through a drop-down menu. At this writing, the industry is waiting for a plethora of commercial packages to soon be available. Without these navigation tools, one can easily become lost in cyberspace.

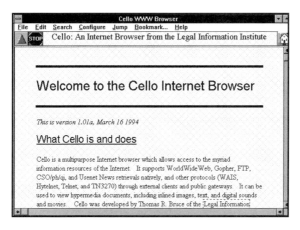

Figure 3—Cello/WWW Browser

One can access Internet in various ways. Most colleges and universities provide access for their faculty and students. Commercial services such as America Online and others are providing gateways to Internet through their services. Also, one can sign up for access through a commercial vendor. These vendors have various pricing structures, some charging by connect time, others by monthly fee, and still others by a combination of methods. In some cities, public and private libraries provide access to Internet for their patrons. Microsoft plans to offer full access to Internet as part of its Microsoft Network on-line service.

Once connected, one can use three of the most empowering applications—e-mail, bulletin boards, and conferences.

ELECTRONIC COMMUNICATIONS APPLICATIONS

The explosive growth of the use of e-mail, bulletin boards, and conference applications can be attributed to the dramatic price drops in hardware and software, to software that is easy to use, and to the competitive advantage that users have over non-users.

E-mail. The dramatic growth of the use of e-mail is documented in the graph below. In addition to the main reasons listed above, businesses and private individuals use e-mail for several other reasons. One, of course, is cost. E-mail saves handling, paper, and postage costs. While some commercial services charge for e-mail after a certain maximum number of messages have been sent, the cost per message or page is still less than U.S. postage rates. Another benefit is instant delivery of messages to the receiver's mailbox. This feature makes it superior to fax since the message sits in the receiver's private mailbox, not in a fax tray for anyone to inspect.

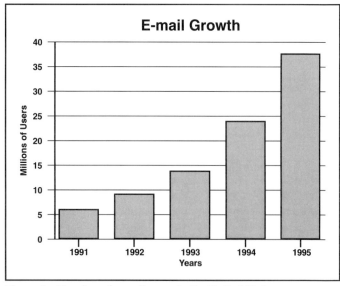

Figure 4—Number of e-mail users in the United States

One company, Verifone, prefers e-mail to p-mail (their term for paper mail) and encourages its customers to communicate with them this way. In fact, paper is even banned internally. Managers at Verifone average 60 messages a day on the company's mail system and the Internet. They believe it enhances their ability to compete effectively and to continue projects 24 hours a day by passing them from time zone to time zone. This competitive strategy enabled the company to present a proposal to a German bank within days, leaving its competitors behind. In this case, the company gained over 80 percent of the business (Freedman, 1993).

The White House has also embraced e-mail. Citizens can send e-mail directly to the White House through both the commercial services and the Internet. In fact, the White House now receives about 800 e-mail messages a day and expects the number to grow. It also expects to be receiving messages with graphics and video components soon (Chapman, 1993).

Other users of e-mail cite convenience and productivity as major reasons they prefer e-mail. E-mail can be sent any time of day from nearly anywhere a system allows a connection. Receivers of messages who are not interrupted from work can be more productive at their jobs.

New products make using e-mail easy. Many software application programs are now e-mail enabled, allowing a user on a network simply to click a button or select a command to mail a word processing document or a spreadsheet. Furthermore, products like MailPlus and Microsoft's new mail client in Windows 95 let users of multiple e-mail systems use one common interface to send, receive, and manage e-mail. The most popular e-mail software programs are: cc:Mail, Microsoft Mail, and WordPerfect Office.

As more users have e-mail access, more business can be conducted by e-mail. Therefore, many reasons seem to be contributing to the growth of this technology. Helping students to learn and feel comfortable using the technology is the first job. The second job is helping students learn to use it effectively. Some ideas for doing this are presented in the following section.

IMPLEMENTATION OF CONNECTED TECHNOLOGIES

Bulletin boards. Bulletin boards refer broadly to any place where information is posted for others to read or where files are stored for others to use. Their use in business is growing rapidly, but their nature varies widely. Some are individually run bulletin board systems (BBSs), set up with a computer and shareware; others are professionally done; and still others are run on commercial services. Today's bulletin board systems can be configured to assure security of data and to check for viruses. Some of the most popular BBS software for DOS computers are PC Board, TBBS (The Bread Board System), The Major BBS, and Wildcat (Wood, 1993).

Some businesses today consider bulletin boards essential tools. Many of these businesses are software companies that run technical user-support bulletin boards, or hardware companies with new products that provide users access to technical support 24 hours a day (Wood, 1993). Some companies also distribute software upgrades or interim releases of programs online. Microsoft, for example, made its upgrade to DOS 6.2 and made new releases of its

File Manager available free online.

Other companies are beginning to use bulletin boards as a way to serve their customers more fully. One car salesperson set up a BBS to advertise the latest models in his dealership's inventory (Harrer, 1993). Still other companies are using bulletin boards to keep a sales force informed of new products, pricing, and policies. Seagate Technology posts customers' most frequently asked questions along with Seagate's responses. This feature alone can save numerous phone calls and give customers the information they need. A BBS is viewed by companies as one of the least expensive product support systems, and customers get responses to their inquiries much faster than by fax or a letter.

In addition to accessing BBSs set up by individual companies, one can also find numerous bulletin boards on both commercial services and the Internet. Those on commercial services are usually set up by subject area, but most services will rent space for private boards, too. Internet also has an area for bulletin boards, called Usenet. Usenet was intended to be a way for people to have electronic discussions; these discussion groups are now referred to as newsgroups.

Newsgroups can cover topics ranging from technical computer topics to religious philosophies. A user can read items posted, respond to items, or create a newsgroup. Small businesses often find the experts they need in these newsgroups. However, these discussion groups differ from conferences in that the responses are not in "real time" (at the same time). This means that a comment posted on a bulletin board may get a good response immediately or it may take several postings to get an appropriate response.

Many schools post information on a BBS. These postings contain information on such topics as library hours, exam schedules, school calendars, course listings, and faculty information. Some universities have departments with BBSs that are regularly accessed by students and alumni alike.

An exceptional feature of bulletin boards is that of being a place to organize and archive information for use when needed. Instead of sending out an e-mail notice to a distribution list of students or teachers, a sender can post it so those who need and want to see it can access it at any time.

E-mail and BBSs can complement each other. For example, an e-mail message could be sent to everyone on a distribution list letting them know that a job opening is posted on the electronic bulletin board. Those who are interested can access the information; others can delete the announcement from their mailboxes.

Bulletin boards can be a useful tool for businesses and individuals who need to gather, share, and distribute information in a timely fashion. This technology gives people access to information when they need it.

Conferences. Conferencing refers to communicating with others at different and maybe distant locations at the same time, which is referred to as real-time. A variety of conferencing software products can run on networks. Newer programs incorporate video and audio as well as text and graphics. This technology enables businesses to bring people of different expertise together without the time and cost of getting them together physically.

Commercial services frequently offer conferences with experts, in which nonexperts can question the experts. These conferences often save the text for reading at a later time.

Conferencing is used over networks or telephone lines in businesses to create statements or policies that need a corporate voice. For example, in a crisis situation a company must respond quickly and accurately. Through real-time conferencing, participants in the conference can agree on a statement that best reflects a corporate position. If consistent policies across an organization with distant locations are desired, managers at the locations could create these policies together in a real-time conference.

No matter which of these applications one uses, online etiquette is expected at all times. Some guidelines for electronic etiquette are presented in Figure 5.

Electronic Etiquette*

Know your recipient
Be respectful
Control emotional outbursts
Use humor with care
Use common English
Use cute symbols sparingly
Don't shout (Use all CAPS)
Remember that you are on record
Be succinct
Limit your message distribution to must haves
Don't be pushy
Be upfront about copies
Identify yourself and your subject clearly
Remember messages can be saved and forwarded
Don't overuse "urgent" or "priority"
Use the receipt requested feature sparingly
Read your e-mail
Use e-mail whenever possible

* Also called "netiquette." Adapted from Larry Magid's posting on Prodigy.

Figure 5—Basic Manners for Online Communications

INSTRUCTIONAL USES FOR CONNECTED TECHNOLOGIES

Because these technologies are becoming standard tools for gathering, sharing, and distributing information in the business environment, using these technologies to learn these information processing skills is becoming more important. The following section presents ideas for integrating (not teaching) e-mail, bulletin boards, and conferences in business classes and some potential benefits.

Electronic mail activities and benefits

Activity: Have students send the teacher messages at the beginning of the semester telling what they expect to get from the class.

Benefits:

- The teacher can double check to be sure that students can use the system correctly.
- The teacher learns to tailor the class to meet most students' expectations.

Activity: Assign group projects where collaborative efforts are required for students to plan projects and communicate with each other using e-mail.

Benefits:

- The instructor will be spared numerous questions from students since many students prefer to ask for clarification from classmates rather than from the instructor.
- E-mail can encourage students to feel more positive about interactions with both classmates and instructors.
- Groups who have conflicting schedules get their projects done without inconveniencing others.
- Planning and communications increase among students in groups.
- Instructors can monitor student progress.
- Instructors can use e-mail to remind students of timetables or deadlines.
- Rapport is developed among students.
- Students are exposed to the work of their peers.

Activity: Assign information gathering tasks similar to those on the job to develop skills for gathering hard-to-find information.

Benefits:

- Using cases such as the one below helps students develop the basic skills for writing a standard inquiry letter. It gives students an opportunity to work on organizing information, stating questions clearly, supplying appropriate details, and creating goodwill.
- Students practice critical thinking when they are required to solicit information not available through printed sources.
- Students gather primary (first-hand) information for reports. Students are encouraged to write to authors of articles or editors of journals, who invite responses by publishing their e-mail addresses.
- Students can be required to keep an electronic journal for writing exercises, article critiques, or summaries.

As the technology develops to include mail with compound documents (text and video or audio), numerous other assignments or variations of these can be developed.

Your company appointed you coordinator for next year's annual sales meeting. As usual, it will be held in August. One of the locations the board of directors wants you to investigate is [insert receiver's location]. You remember that [insert student name], one of the company's most competent sales representatives, lives in the area. You decide to send an inquiry to [him/her] asking about the area's potential for the meeting. This information will be used to write a report.

Ask those questions which will elicit the answers you need to write your report and support your recommendation to the board. You want your inquiry to cover the basics as well as give you an insider's view of the area. You want more than you could get from travel guides or the local chamber of commerce.

Your report should include but not be limited to customs, business dress, food, transportation, excursions, taboos, entertainment, typical weather, and temperature. Feel free to add any details you need as long as you do not change the basic nature of the case. Your company's directory lists [insert student's name]'s Internet address as [insert Internet address]. Be sure to save a copy of your message for your records.

Figure 6—Case for e-mail Usage

Bulletin board activities and benefits

Activity: Have students post brief autobiographies on the class bulletin board or a section of a bulletin board devoted to the class.

Benefits:

- The instructor can evaluate students on their ability to post and read from the system.
- Instructors can develop a good rapport with students while learning about them through their autobiographies.
- Groupwork improves when members believe they understand the backgrounds of their team members.
- Students often develop new friendships by discovering others in their class with similar interests or backgrounds.

Activity: Create topics on the bulletin board so that students can exchange ideas on both personal and communications topics.

Benefits:

- This encourages use of the technology, making students more comfortable with it as a tool for information gathering, sharing, and distribution.
- Students are encouraged to read and think about a variety of topics.

Activity: Post information about activities on campus or about class assignments.

Benefits:

- Posting information about assignments will save time for students and instructors alike.

- Posting information on scholarships, interviews, lectures, good movies, and television programs can build goodwill among students and instructors.

Activity: Assign information-gathering tasks typical of business employees and have students use the Internet gophers to locate information.

Benefits:

- Students may locate books on particular topics in the Library of Congress, get help with a particular software problem, find elegant but quaint dining places in a distant city to take a client for business purposes, or get the weather report for a particular area where one is traveling.

- Students may gather information from Edgar, the SEC's Electronic Gathering and Retrieval System, on a particular company. The instructor should limit the time for data gathering or choose a listing so new that the information can only be found online.

If one has free access to commercial services or can budget for information-gathering activities, numerous real-world tasks can be practiced by students.

Conferences

Activity: Discuss e-mail etiquette.

Benefits:

- This activity creates an awareness that there is an acceptable social behavior online and allows students to discuss possible reasons for such manners.

- Students become aware that different forms of media have different cultures with different expectations.

- Students may be encouraged to listen and observe some conferences to learn the "rules" to avoid getting cut off by others for inappropriate behavior.

Activity: Discuss an assigned reading for the class.

Benefits:

- Allows all students to participate when they might not in a class for various reasons, such as limited time, shyness, absence, or fear of peer or teacher reactions.

- Gives students an opportunity to see that there can be many perspectives on a single reading.

Activity: Assign a business task, such as writing a policy for posting on the company BBS.

Benefits:

- Students will recognize this as a useful business tool.

- Students practice collaborative writing.

With the flexibility of today's conferencing software, instructors can allow students to hold these conferences at times and places convenient for all participants, not necessarily in a face-to-face classroom setting.

IMPLICATIONS FOR THE FUTURE

In the future one may not read NBEA Yearbooks in print. In fact, books may even become collectibles. Instead one will sign on to the professional online bulletin board, supported by dues or subscribed to on a per-use basis. Not only will the yearbook always be available, but colorful graphics, sound, and perhaps even video will be a part of the yearbooks. One may be able to interact with it or at least leave comments for others to see and answer. Instructors will be connected to others teaching similar classes, solving similar problems, and working with similar students. One will be able to share assignments, perspectives, and ideas. This may be done publicly through multimedia BBSs and privately with multimedia e-mail.

Not only are these technologies reshaping our work cultures, but they are paving the way for the next generation of workgroup software. Workgroup software allows groups to work on projects together but not necessarily at the same time or in the same location. Workgroup software will further alter our work structure and possibly boost productivity. For example, when workgroup software is used by several instructors to create multimedia presentations for classroom use, the workgroup software will help members schedule conferences, access databases, and manage the work flow (Reinhardt, 1993).

Futurists predict that those most likely to benefit on this electronic frontier will be "content providers," those who write books, organize information, and create the video and sound presentations. Since there is an enormous market for entertainment (Stewart, 1993), the entertainment industry is expected to pay for much of the future application development.

In the future, connected technologies will be easier to use, have common interfaces making it easier to learn, and be less expensive. Connectedness will enhance the teaching/learning environment as well as our lives.

REFERENCES

Chapman, G. (July 1993). Sending a message to the White House. *Technology Review*, p. 16-17.

Freedman, D. H. (Autumn 1993). Culture of urgency. *Forbes ASAP*. p. 25-28.

Harrer, J. (March 1993). Bulletin board systems are beginning to emerge in business applications. *Telecommunications*. p. 58-59.

Reinhardt, A. (March 1993). Smarter e-mail is coming. *Byte*. p. 90.

Rodriguez, K. (August 22, 1994). Marvel to be announced in fall. *Infoworld*. p. 5.

Stewart, T. A. (Autumn 1993). Boom time on the new frontier. *Fortune*. p. 158.

Tetzelli, R. (March 7, 1994). The Internet and your business. *Fortune*. p. 92.

van Kirk, D. (August 22, 1994). Chicago opens mail options. *Infoworld*. p. 6.

Wood, L. (May 1, 1993). Business profits from bulletin boards. *Datamation*. pp. 45-58.

CHAPTER 9

Interactive Television in the Classroom

PATRICIA SAVAGE

Peabody High School, Peabody, Kansas

People often dream of appearing on television. Stop for a moment and visualize yourself on television. How would you appear? What would your body language, gestures, and voice be like? For educators, the dream of appearing on television has become reality; it's called interactive television!

GENERAL DESCRIPTION OF INTERACTIVE TELEVISION

"Interactive television (ITV) is a telecommunications system that permits students and teachers to see, hear, and communicate with one another simultaneously" (Project Interact, 1992). It is often referred to as distance learning or interactive video. ITV provides the ability to see and hear people in different locations with no pause in video or audio. New technology has allowed educators to link classrooms together electronically that are several miles apart physically.

With interactive TV, a teacher can teach a class in one location but have students in several other locations. All students can see, hear, and talk to the teacher and to students at the other sites. To do this, enough TV monitors must be in each location so that the teacher and students can view the other locations. For example, if five locations are viewing the class, each location should have four monitors for students to watch and four monitors for the teacher to watch. The classroom that has the teacher in it does not need a monitor to view itself.

The media used to transmit the video and audio is usually fiber optic cable or twisted pair phone wires. Sometimes the transmission media is owned by the schools involved or it is leased from a telephone company or other private business. Cameras and microphones are other essential elements in each of the ITV classrooms. One camera in each classroom must be focused on students and one on the teacher. Microphones are needed by the teacher and by each student in each classroom.

Today, interactive TV is bringing many changes to teaching methods and to course offerings. Educators have always played an important role in technological advancements. Although some educators within a school system are probably not involved with technology as much as are business and computer teachers, interactive television is an avenue for all teachers to be involved with technology.

For ITV to be a success, teachers must feel comfortable with the equipment.

Therefore, training on the ITV system is very important. Teachers must also become educated about the setup, instructional techniques, and the benefits of teaching on an ITV system.

ITV is a very expensive technology and requires skilled technicians to install. Because of the expense, some schools join together to form an ITV consortium so that the cost of equipment and teacher salaries can be allocated among five to eight school districts.

ITV BENEFITS AND ADVANTAGES

To keep school districts with low enrollments alive and well, some areas in the United States must either consolidate small school districts to compete effectively with larger metropolitan school districts or they must adopt technology to provide equal access to the instruction that larger school districts provide through larger course offerings. Interactive television may be one solution to keep our small, rural school districts alive.

Large school districts can also benefit from ITV. They can offer nontypical courses such as Japanese to students in several districts via ITV. And large districts with specialized teachers in foreign languages or science can offer their courses via ITV to smaller districts that could not afford to offer those courses.

The following section describes a number of benefits for students, the school, and the community that are willing to use ITV.

Student benefits. ITV provides many benefits for students. It allows courses to be offered even though qualified teachers are scarce. Hughes (1988) reported that ITV has been successful in small school districts in solving the problems of insufficient enrollment in classes and inadequate staffing. Many graduates of rural school districts will testify that their school curriculum did not meet their needs. By offering courses via ITV, students are able to select from a greater variety of classes. Schools can offer advanced classes such as Discrete Math, Anatomy and Physiology, or Economics using ITV.

Another benefit of ITV (Piirto, 1993) is that it breaks down the barriers of time and distance, meeting people's needs for convenience and quality in education. Students also benefit from the social interaction and communication with teachers and students in other sites. This breaks down some of the rivalry barriers that sometimes exist between school districts in rural areas. Students feel that classes taught on ITV systems involve higher level learning. The classes seem to encourage more discussion, teamwork, and problem solving, whereas a regular classroom may consist of lecture and notetaking (Schmidt and Patton, March 1994).

A final benefit for students is their active participation in the use of new technologies. Before students can feel comfortable in an interactive television classroom, they must be comfortable with the technological environment. Students, as well as teachers, need to be comfortable when working with the equipment. Therefore, equipment training is essential.

School benefits. ITV classrooms provide many benefits for the school district. As stated earlier, schools can offer a greater variety of classes, but the most appealing part is that no new teachers need to be hired. ITV is perfect for classes that have high demand by students but a low supply of qualified teachers. An example of this would be foreign language classes. Some small, rural school districts can justify hiring only one foreign language teacher. Even large school districts may find it difficult to hire someone to teach Japanese or a Chinese language. Through the ITV system, students can learn different languages taught by instructors in other schools.

School districts can benefit by providing in-service training for school board members, administrators, teachers, staff, and bus drivers through the ITV system and save time and travel expenses.

Community and business benefits. Community members, organizations, and business leaders can also benefit by using ITV systems. Service organizations can hold area meetings and save on travel expenses and time. College courses can be offered to the community through ITV. This may give adults more incentive to begin a college education.

A hidden benefit of the ITV system is that it can bring the community, businesses, and the school system closer together. By using ITV, community members and business leaders may understand its potential and become more involved with education in general. Because of the cost of ITV equipment, schools should encourage outsiders to use it and they should charge a reasonable usage fee.

ITV PROBLEMS AND CONSTRAINTS

With most new technologies, problems and constraints exist. ITV systems are no different. In an evaluation of ITV in Minnesota, Morehouse (1987) noted a few inherent disadvantages, including a greater frequency of cheating, lack of personal contact with students, movement and space restrictions, occasional technical problems, delays in material transfer, and conflicting school calendars and daily schedules.

A few other problems can be encountered. First, selecting and training faculty to use the equipment can be difficult. Faculty members chosen to teach with ITV must be dedicated enough to attend training sessions dealing with effective and ineffective ITV techniques. Usually, a good teacher will become a better teacher when using ITV, but a poor teacher will be blatantly poor.

Second, enrollment in ITV classes must be limited. The number will depend on the size of the classroom and the ability of the equipment to view all students. In most small, rural school districts, this will not be a problem because of small school enrollment numbers. In community colleges or universities that want to hold large classes, this can be a problem. ITV teaching methodologies encourage a lot of student participation and interaction. Large classes do not lend themselves to this type of interaction and can quickly degrade into the talking head syndrome—watching a teacher's head on the TV monitor.

A final problem is that students at the reception site may be left unattended. To combat that problem, some school district consortiums have created student conduct policies. Each student and his/her parents must sign the policy that states the expected behavior from the students and the disciplinary action to be taken. An example of a student enrollment contract from the Technology Excellence Education Network (TEEN) Consortium (Talge, 1994) follows:

TEEN STUDENT ENROLLMENT CONTRACT

All TEEN students will indicate their understanding and acceptance of the TEEN Student Code of Conduct policy by signing the form below. Parent or guardian signature(s) are also required as a means of assuring they are aware of the standards expected of students enrolling in the TEEN course offerings.

Student Name_____Grade Level_____
School of Official Enrollment _____
Parent or Guardian_____ Telephone_____
TEEN Course(s) _____

Student Code of Conduct Policy

As the undersigned student of record in a TEEN course, I understand and accept the Student Code of Conduct Policy and agree to abide by the policies and procedures established by the Governing Board of TEEN. I agree that:

1. Insubordination of any kind (behaviors or happenings that disrupt or interfere with teaching or learning) will not be tolerated in TEEN classrooms;

2. Language or gestures generally agreed upon as suggestive, derogatory, or abusive in nature will not be tolerated;

3. I can be recorded (visual or audio) at any time without specific pre-warning;

4. I will position myself in the classroom to be in camera view at all times;

5. I will not manipulate equipment in the classroom without express direction from supervisors or instructors;

6. I will conform to any additional rules as specified orally or in writing by the instructor.

Further, I understand that if I am found to be in violation of any policies listed above, I will be subject to the following disciplinary action:

First Offense: Verbal or written warning from instructor followed by parental notification of the infraction through written letter. The warning will be delivered to the students using procedures that assure student privacy. A copy of the letter will also be sent to the students' principal.

Second Offense: The student will be removed from the class until such time that a conference of parents, student, instructor, and principal offers assurance that the misconduct will not reoccur.

**Severe Misconduct, including damage or defacing TEEN equipment or facilities, threats, violent behavior or intent, or repeated policy violation, including drug, alcohol, or narcotic policy violation may result in permanent removal from the class. The student may be subject to loss of full or partial credit of coursework.

This TEEN enrollment contract does not supersede policies or provisions for student conduct recognized by the student's place of official enrollment.

_____
Student Signature   Date

_____
Parent Signature   Date

_____
Principal   Date

Most problems with ITV school district consortiums can be solved with preparation, organization, and reliable faculty.

ROLES OF INDIVIDUALS INVOLVED WITH ITV

To help alleviate some of the constraints of interactive television, a complete understanding of the roles of the student, teacher, and the facilitator is needed.

Students' roles. Students enrolled in ITV courses should be screened by guidance counselors or principals. The student is expected to go above and beyond the regular class requirements. Students must be able to remain focused on course content at ALL times, and they must play an aggressive role in providing interaction and feedback.

ITV places more demands on students than traditional classrooms. Students must feel comfortable with using the interactive television delivery system. Additionally, they must show maturity, responsibility, and discipline to do the daily work and the homework. Students must be able to meet these demands prior to enrollment in ITV classes. This is one way school districts can limit the enrollment in ITV classes.

Instructors' roles. The teacher's role must be altered when using ITV as follows:

1. Teachers must become familiar with the technological system. They must be able to navigate the cameras and monitors using control buttons.

2. Teachers should try to make the students feel as comfortable as possible. They must remember the technology is new to the students also.

3. Instruction should be adapted to meet the needs of the students. To know the needs of students, teachers must make sure they are familiar with their students and the students are familiar with each other (Distance Education, 1989).

Facilitator's role. The responsibilities of a facilitator are different for each ITV operation. Some schools have a full-time facilitator who stays in the room the entire day and/or evening. Other consortiums use part-time facilitators who are in the school all day but are not in the ITV classroom. Part-time facilitators are usually a counselor, librarian, secretary, or another teacher. Responsibilities are similar for both types of facilitators.

The main responsibility of a facilitator includes maintenance and use of equipment. This may include checking the equipment every day and troubleshooting it, setting up the room for instruction when substitute teachers are used, and contacting a technician when necessary. The facilitator also becomes a liaison between personnel at one site and directors, principals, and teachers at remote sites.

A pre-designed system of communication is essential to make sure that course materials are provided to each student prior to each class session. Wedel (1994) described her facilitator job as being in charge of receiving, sending, and copying student material, student grades, and progress reports. Facilitators are a critical link to making an ITV consortium run smoothly. The ideal system is to have copies of all handouts and tests prepared, copied, and sent to all sites before the school year or semester begins. Otherwise, one must rely on the Postal Service, faxes, and overnight delivery services—services that can become very expensive.

INSTRUCTIONAL TECHNIQUES AND TIPS

The instructional methods necessary for teaching on ITV systems are comparable to the regular classroom, with a few adjustments. The quality of instruction will be determined by how well the instructor can adapt his/her teaching style to an ITV system. Training sessions need to be given to instructors by experienced ITV teachers.

Teaching methods. New technology does not always work properly, and teachers must turn the little mishaps that occur to their advantage and always stay calm. This technology often demands that a teacher have a good sense of humor (Interactive Television, 1988). The Kansas State Board of Education (1992) offers several instructional tips for teaching on ITV:

1. Relax.
2. Present information as you would in a traditional classroom, with a few modifications.
3. Be organized.
4. Be prepared in advance.
5. Give a clear presentation and concise instructions.
6. Use clear, well produced audio-video aids.
7. Talk slowly and clearly.
8. Make the students in remote sites feel part of the class by maintaining eye contact with the camera.
9. Move the camera to the student asking the question.
10. Pay attention to your appearance.
11. Smile.

Interaction methods. Interaction is a very important communication tool on the ITV system. There are three basic forms of interaction: instructor to student, student to instructor, and student to student. An ITV classroom should have all three forms of interaction. The following are some suggestions to help implement better interaction:

• Have a student answer a question from another student instead of the instructor.
• Assign students oral reading from a textbook.
• Have students work in groups on a project or case problem and make a presentation. Each student should be in charge of a portion of the presentation.

Personalizing instruction. Using technology may make a lesson seem very distant. An important part of ITV teaching is personalizing the lesson. In a regular classroom, teachers use individualized instruction and reinforcement methods such as a "pat on the back." ITV teachers must find similar techniques to personalize their lessons. Some suggestions for personalizing a lesson include:

1. Call students by name and avoid stating the school site. This will create a feeling of having one class.
2. Put questions related to the class on an overhead camera as students are arriving. This will help focus the attention of all students on a common item.
3. Visit remote sites and take your home-site students along. Let the students meet each other personally.
4. Have students introduce themselves in front of the teacher-focused camera.
5. Give a quiz every day for the first week using information about the students.
6. Plan a few minutes of social interaction between sites. Allow students a few minutes to ask about sporting events, proms, homecoming, etc.

7. Have students share information not only about themselves, but their schools.

8. Insist that all students learn the names of students in all sites.

With all the instructional modifications that need to be made with ITV instruction, the question "Is instruction on ITV equal to that of a traditional classroom?" is often asked. Having a teacher be there in person and able to work with students on a one-on-one basis seems to be a very effective instructional method in traditional classrooms. While traditional classrooms have advantages over ITV classrooms, ITV systems have advantages over traditional classrooms. For example, when a student is absent from a traditional classroom, the student misses an important lecture or discussion that can only be made up by copying notes from another student. When using ITV systems, a tape can be inserted into a VCR, and a class lecture can be recorded. Students can watch the tape at a later date, thereby not missing a crucial lecture or student discussion.

Classroom equipment. The ideal classroom would combine the best technology for transmission and reception. (Dufriend, 1994). Classroom equipment will vary depending on the existing building and rooms available for ITV instruction. However, the ideal ITV classroom specifications are outlined as follows:

- The room size should be about 24 feet X 30 feet with carpet on three walls.
- The ceiling should be at least 12 feet high.
- Air conditioner and heating controls should be separate from the rest of the building in order to control background noise.
- The classroom should have its own dedicated telephone line for a fax machine. The fax machine should be a plain paper machine that is also a copier, computer printer, and a scanner.
- The classroom should contain four or five 27-inch television monitors (depending on the size of the ITV consortium) hanging from the ceiling for teacher viewing, and the same number of 32-inch television monitors for student viewing of students at the other sites.
- Two video cameras should be mounted—one to view the class and another to view the instructor.
- The instructor's camera should follow the instructor at the instructor's desk. Cameraman is one device that allows the instructor to move back and forth in front of the class rather than standing in one location only.
- The instructor's desk should contain an overhead camera (ELMO), a monitor, computer workstation, and a control panel.
- The teacher's microphone should be wireless.
- Student areas should contain tables and chairs along with a computer at each station. Student microphones should be attached to the tables with one microphone per student, and they should be "directional" (Dufriend, 1994).

Equipment in ITV classrooms may vary. For example, some classrooms may not have computers for every student or for any students. ITV equipment will depend on the budget in terms of the quantities and types of ITV equipment utilized.

Cost. The primary concern for many people is the cost of the equipment, installation charges, and usage charges. Prices may vary depending on the number of schools involved, the number of students, and the equipment purchased. The costs that follow reflect the expenses of the newest consortium in Kansas, which is the TEEN (Technology Excellence Education Network) consortium.

Five schools are involved in the TEEN consortium. The system was used for the first time in the fall of 1993. According to Wedel (1994), the cost for one classroom of equipment at one site for a five-school consortium was approximately $40,000. The total cost, including laying fiber optic cable, for this five-school consortium was approximately $800,000. This cost was divided equally among the five school districts, for a cost of $160,000 each. The consortium borrowed the money and plans to pay it back over a five year period.

This consortium laid fiber optic cable to connect the five school districts. By owning its own ITV network, the consortium will be able to expand the network's uses to include sharing of library resources and computer software. When consortiums lease their network media (cabling) from telephone companies, they have no control over price increases on telephone bills and may find it difficult to continue with the service if charges become excessive. Another benefit of owning all the equipment rather than leasing it is that the consortium can make money off the ITV network by charging businesses to use it.

BUSINESS CLASSES VIA ITV

Where do business classes fit in an ITV system? According to Torgerson (1994), who has taught a business course on ITV, it is the ideal method to teach high level business classes such as Economics, Business Management, International Business, and Entrepreneurship in secondary schools. Many small school districts employ one full-time business teacher, restricting course offerings such as International Business if only a few students are interested in taking it. But, if two or three students from each of five sites are interested in International Business, one can justify teaching it over an ITV system. This is a big advantage for business students in small school districts.

At the university level, as enrollments decline in schools of business, administrators have found that they can offer one section of a course but have it transmitted to two or more sites. One class could be on campus and the other could be for employees at a specific business. Or, the instructor may teach one class on campus but have students located in two or three other sites either within the state or out of state.

ITV can save the instructor a great amount of traveling time and save travel expenses for the institution. At this point, the cost of providing ITV instruction is so high that tuition will not cover the added expenses. Some ITV classes have additional fees charged because of the additional costs. At this time, ITV is a new instructional delivery method that has a value that cannot be attached to a dollar amount.

SUMMARY

Interactive television has become the new method of delivering instruction. Like any other new technology it has its advantages and disadvantages; however, the advantages outweigh the disadvantages. ITV can enhance and enrich the curriculum of many educational institutions and provide services for the community as well. Because of its complexity and cost, communication, planning, training, and dedication are needed to make it a success.

REFERENCES

Distance education teaching tips at a glance. (1989). Alaska University, Anchorage, Alaska.

Dufriend, C. (1994, February). Technical Support Director, TEEN Consortium.

Hughes, A. (1988, April). The crisis of distance learning—A dangerous opportunity. Paper presented at the 1992 AERA Annual Meeting.

Interactive television teaching—Integrating technology series. (1988). Minnesota State Department of Education, St. Paul, MN.

Lundgren, R. W. (1985). Two-way television in rural curriculum development. *NASSP Bulletin*, 12, 19.

Morehouse, D. L. (1987). Analysis based on the evaluation of Minnesota's technology demonstration program. Minnesota State Department of Education, St. Paul, MN.

Piirto, R. (1993). Teaching on television. *American Demographics*, 9, 6.

Project INTERACT – Interactive television technical operations and communications skills training manual. (1992). Kansas State Board of Education, Topeka, KS.

Schmidt, E. & Patton, R. (1994, March). (Personal interview about ITV students).

Tatge, S. (1994, February). (Personal interview with a technical support director).

Torgerson, B. (1994, March). (Personal interview with an economics ITV teacher).

Wedel, J. (1994, March). (Personal interview with an ITV facilitator).

PART III

Evaluating Instructional Technology
For Classroom Application

LISA E. GUELDENZOPH
DAVID J. HYSLOP
Bowling Green State University
Bowling Green, Ohio

Evaluating technology for instructional use is an important process. The decisions that are made will affect teachers and students for many years, and a good decision can impact instructional effectiveness in a variety of ways. The process of evaluating technology is also very complex; it involves many factors and, in some cases, involves a number of teachers and administrators. Whoever conducts the evaluation process will need to identify and understand the many variables which impact the final decision.

The purpose of this chapter is to summarize the primary considerations that are part of the process of evaluating hardware and software and present guidelines to help make this process easier and more effective. Some general guidelines for evaluating technology are presented first, and then more specific guidelines for hardware and software considerations are presented later in the chapter.

When trying to delineate the most significant factors which should be analyzed, one should note the dynamics of this decision-making process. As new technology is developed and information processes change—as is occurring at an ever-increasing rate—the process of evaluating this technology for instructional use is dynamic and outdated quickly, if not continuously changed.

CRITERIA FOR EVALUATING INSTRUCTIONAL TECHNOLOGY

Technology is an important tool for improving instructional design and effectiveness. To maximize its effectiveness, a number of criteria should be considered before hardware or software is integrated into the classroom. One of the most important elements to evaluate is the role that technology assumes in creating or enhancing classroom learning activities and, eventually, developing student competencies which meet workplace expectations. As noted by Lambrecht (1987), "the fundamental question to answer before selecting any software or hardware is what students are to be taught: What are the goals— the expected outcomes—of the instructional program?"

Instructional technology can create learning situations which result in a high degree of transfer of learning from the classroom to the job. Instructional techniques such as simulations, drills, or tutorials can be effectively developed using software packages in most computer application courses. Most other courses can also use technology in a variety of learning situations. The important concept to follow, however, is to ensure that the technology application meets the business or workplace standard. An important criterion when completing the evaluation process is to determine current job expectations or workplace standards; this requires a careful assessment of job competencies by employers.

Cost considerations. A significant element in the purchase and adoption of instructional technology is cost. Although evaluating instructional technology involves both financial and nonfinancial considerations, in many cases the cost of technology will determine what is selected for instructional use even though it should not be the most important selection criterion. Hardware and software that are not selling well in the business world are sometimes sold to schools at a tremendous discount. Choosing this type of hardware or software is not a wise decision if a secondary or postsecondary school's goal is to teach students on the same type of hardware and software being used in businesses.

Frequently, teachers should conduct comparative analyses of different brands (and features) of technology including costs such as service contracts and maintenance agreements. Other areas that should be compared include upgrade options and costs, trade in or residual value, and leasing vs. purchasing. All of these areas should be examined to determine price differences.

Standardization within institutions. Most educational institutions have developed policies which standardize the purchase and use of technology within their organizations. Having such policies helps to control costs, enhances connectivity between equipment, minimizes training needs, and maximizes sharing of concerns and experiences by staff. By using similar equipment, teachers can achieve a high degree of instructional effectiveness by collaborating on the creation of learning activities. Furthermore, formal training on the use of the technology can be developed and administered very effectively if staff have common learning needs due to the use of similar technology. Instructional support, whether provided by a specialist within the school, specific teachers, or vendors, can be more easily provided when the technology is common throughout the institution.

Use of appropriate technology. The development and use of instructional objectives can help to guide the use of technology. As learning objectives for a class or unit of instruction are developed, technology can be analyzed to see how it can be used to maximize student learning. In this context, technology can help in developing learning activities such as drills, tutorials, simulations, and other instructional techniques. An important criterion to consider, therefore, is the degree to which the technology relates to achieving the learning objectives in a course or as part of a program of study. When comparing a number of similar products, some differentiation of features is usually present. By reviewing these features, certain products can be determined to be more appropriate for achieving the learning objectives.

Use of an evaluation plan. A number of criteria for evaluating the use of technology can be developed for use by decision makers at any institution. Some of the general criteria can be developed as part of a cost-benefit analysis described in the next section of this chapter. As an evaluation plan is developed, it is important that the plan be completed in collaboration with the key personnel within the institution who are responsible for deciding the type of technology that is purchased and adopted for classroom use.

Teachers exercise a critical role in developing the plan since they will be responsible for implementing and evaluating the effectiveness of the technology. However, other personnel within the institution may also assume an important role in this process and should be included in the formulation of a plan. For example, administrators are responsible for the institution's academic programs and financial well-being and will have an important role in evaluating technology and making decisions. Likewise, individuals responsible for instructional support (such as technology administrators or equipment supervisors) will also be directly impacted by decisions regarding technology; thus they should also be included in the evaluation process.

PLANNING THE EVALUATION PROCESS

Evaluating technology requires that several specific steps be completed prior to implementation of the technology. These steps include conducting a needs analysis, completing a cost-benefit analysis, and constructing a plan to determine how the implementation of technology eventually will be evaluated to assess its role and effectiveness.

Conducting a needs analysis. Before the evaluation process begins, a comprehensive needs analysis should be completed. The primary purpose of this needs analysis is to determine how the instructional technology can assist in enhancing learning goals. Internally, the overall mission of the institution could be examined and then program or course goals reviewed to determine the need to adopt or add technology. Within each course, specific learning activities should also be assessed as this is where the technology will have primary impact. A teacher could also review other parts of the instructional program to assure that if new technology is adopted, it will be compatible with existing learning activities.

A needs analysis should also focus on external factors, primarily assessing how the technology will contribute to enhancing students' job and career success. Employers' expectations of needed technological skills can be obtained from a variety of sources. Relevant published information may already be available outlining the technology-related skills and competencies employees should possess for job success. If additional information is desired, surveys can be conducted within a local or regional area to ascertain the skills needed. Informal focus groups could be formed to obtain this information, or business advisory committees could be used. After sufficient information is obtained, then a formal cost-benefit study can be completed.

Designing and completing a cost-benefit study. Designing a cost-benefit analysis requires a comprehensive approach to determine all important variables related to costs and benefits. During this stage, very specific information should be obtained to answer all questions relative to the purchase and use of technology. A cost-benefit analysis can be completed for each type of hardware and/or software being examined and can also be used to compare brands to see which product may have a competitive advantage. For example, while one product may have a competitive price advantage, it may not offer the same level of benefits, thus making price less than the primary consideration.

A number of cost factors can be used to complete this analysis. First, the basic price of the hardware or software can be a starting point and then other cost factors considered. These factors could include:

- service or maintenance agreements
- options to lease or lease with purchase options
- upgrade costs
- trade-in or residual value.

Isolating these costs should be relatively easy by reviewing product literature or talking to the vendor.

The benefit analysis is usually a more subjective, judgmental evaluation than a cost analysis. Benefits should be analyzed in relation to both hardware and software, but they need to focus on how the technology can improve the learning process within the classroom.

The factors to analyze in the benefit analysis include the following:

- compatibility of technology with existing technology
- degree to which technology meets the needs of teachers
- ease of student learning (user friendliness)
- ease of integration with other elements of the learning process
- documentation (how-to manuals) that permits ease of use
- relationship to achievement of student goals
- efficient and effective use of class time
- ease of allowing for teacher's assessment of student performance.

The effective use of technology will help in the design, implementation, and evaluation of a curriculum or course of study. It will serve to reinforce concepts relevant to the learning objectives. It will also enhance the teacher's role in providing well-planned and realistic assignments. As Berger (1993) pointed out, "a computer can help instructors do what they've always done—only better. For example, word-processing software makes it easy to revise course materials and lecture notes to incorporate new information or insights, as well as to make such materials more attractive and accessible."

Completing a follow-up evaluation. The final step in evaluating the use of technology involves determining if the technology improves the learning activities and helps students develop appropriate skills. Although this step is relatively easy to complete, many times it is overlooked or not completed in a comprehensive manner.

To conduct a follow-up evaluation, only two elements are necessary: (a) criteria upon which to conduct the evaluation and (b) a system to measure changes in student learning or performance. Student learning may be measured at the end of a learning activity or be summative—measured at the end of a course or program. There is usually justification for having measurement occur at various times throughout a course, especially if there are wide variances in how technology is used. Teachers can conduct their own evaluation, but they should be careful to include information from students as part of the evaluation process. Once this process is completed, then judgments can be made about altering the use of technology in the classroom, if necessary.

FACTORS AFFECTING HARDWARE USAGE

Determining what comes first, the proverbial chicken (the computer) or the egg (the software), can be confusing. Should an affordable computer system be purchased before choosing the software that will run on that computer? Or should the software be chosen before selecting a computer that will fit the needs of the software? When evaluating technology for classroom applications, the most important factor is selecting technology that meets the instructional needs of the classroom right now and in the next few years. Factors such as money may affect the decision-making process. However, student learning goals should take precedence over other constraints. Regardless of the method used to choose computer technology, several factors exist that will influence the specific technologies that are incorporated into the classroom. As these critical factors are evaluated, consider that the learning process should be emphasized rather than the technology.

Instructional goals/objectives. As the Policies Commission for Business and Economic Education (1993) stated, "the impact of technology is evident in every aspect of society." The primary purpose for incorporating technological advancements into the classroom is to prepare the students for the computerized world that awaits them in both their personal and professional lives. For this reason, it is important for educators to determine the objectives they want their students to reach, especially those objectives that deal most directly with the use of technology. By developing specific objectives, the methods used to meet those objectives can be more easily determined.

IBM vs. Mac. Which hardware platform should be selected—IBM (IBM compatible) or Macintosh? The answer depends on the instructional goals for the program and the objectives for an individual course. One can make a very good case for using Macs to teach desktop publishing or CAD (computer assisted design) becauses businesses use Macs for those purposes. However, IBM compatibles outsell Macs ten to one in the business world so one can make a good case for standardizing on IBM compatibles.

The question of compatibility between the two platforms always arises. Although some sharing of software is possible, IBM and Macintosh products cannot totally support each other's software programs. Even connecting two different types of hardware to a network or two different networks together can be difficult. Today, Macintoshes are more common in elementary schools than in secondary schools, but IBM compatibles have made major inroads in the elementary school marketplace.

Software availability for the two platforms should be considered also. Teachers should review the most popular business programs and the best educational programs and determine whether the programs they want to use are available in versions for IBM compatibles, Macintoshes, or both. At the secondary education level, educators should attempt to provide their students with the technology most appropriate for preparing students for employment.

LANs vs. standalone configurations. Both local area networks (LANs) and standalone computers have advantages and disadvantages. LANs allow users to share software, files, and information among all the computers on the network. Printers and modems are common components within a LAN system. Communication between computers has become very common in the business world today, and students should understand the process of how to use the network effectively. By using a network system in the classroom environment, students will be better prepared for the world of electronic mail and collaborative computing.

When evaluating computer configurations for classroom use, both the traditional network and peer-to-peer networks should be considered. Traditional networks require one computer to be reserved as the file server. This computer acts as the brain for the entire LAN system. The file server cannot be used for individual computing; it is the "Grand Central Station" for the system. The major disadvantage of this type of system is that when a problem occurs with the file server, the entire system fails.

A less powerful LAN system called a peer-to-peer network does not require a file server. Peer-to-peer LANs are usually less expensive than traditional LANs. One of the primary reasons for using a peer-to-peer LAN is to allow many computers to share peripherals such as printers. All computers on the network share the same information and share the responsibility of maintaining the integrity of the system. However, the response time is slower than with a server-based network, especially if the printer is active. Teachers should consider the types of software applications and amount of printing that will be done when selecting a LAN. For example, in a desktop publishing class in which a great amount of printing may be done, the peer-to-peer network may not be a wise choice.

A school that has a peer-to-peer LAN may not need a LAN expert in the school or town whereas a school with a server-based LAN will need to train someone in-house to be a LAN manager and will need a service company in the area that can work on a specific brand of network hardware and software. When a school writes a request for a bid for a LAN, the bid request should include the cost of training two teachers/technicians to install and use the network operating system software and application software, set up directories, set up security on files, and troubleshoot problems.

Overall, server-based LANs handle more tasks, accommodate more users, provide better security for individual users, and process information faster than peer-to-peer systems. A school should evaluate both types of LANs to determine how the learning environment will be affected by implementing either configuration.

As opposed to either network configuration, standalone computer systems provide a sense of security. Each computer possesses its own computer software, its own files, and its own problems. For example, a computer virus would not affect any other standalone computer whereas on a LAN the virus would affect the entire system. However, sharing files or computerized learning activities becomes a tedious task on standalone computers especially if data disks are exchanged among students. Educators must determine the extent to which collaborative computing will be used in the classroom before implementing a specific configuration.

Some application software programs are designed only to run on a network and provide detailed reports on student progress throughout an entire year. These programs can save teachers an immense amount of time grading math or keyboarding assignments, for example, because the assignments are graded automatically.

New models vs. old models. Determining whether to upgrade or stay with a classroom's current technology is a popular debate in many schools. Buying yesterday's technology at low prices means investing in the past! Purchasing the newest technology means investing in the future! By purchasing hardware with large amounts of RAM memory and hard disk space and with a fast microprocessor, a school will be able to keep up with new technological advancements for a longer period of time.

Today's computers are very inexpensive when compared to computers on the market just a few years ago. In many cases, it is difficult to upgrade an older computer without spending nearly the same amount of money for a new system. An advantage of buying new as opposed to upgrading an older model is that every component is replaced at once. It's like buying parts for an old car; once parts are replaced, something else breaks down or becomes obsolete. Sometimes it is better to simply buy a new car.

When deciding whether to buy new technology or upgrade old technology, one needs to consider not only money but also the lifetime of the computer. Whenever any type of technology is purchased, additional time is bought for that piece of equipment. Goodman (1993) suggests that if an older computer is upgraded, the life of that computer is extended by approximately 12 to 18 months; if a new system is purchased, the students will be exposed to at least four years of relevant technology.

Upgradability. If an older computer model is chosen, the machine must be upgradable. As existing software packages are upgraded and new packages are created, more and more RAM memory and hard disk space are needed to run these programs. The larger packages, often incorporating expanded graphic capabilities, become sluggish when run on machines with slow processors. When determining the exact RAM memory and processor specifications, teachers should evaluate the balance between RAM memory requirements and processing speed. RAM memory should be the first consideration.

If several software programs are used to meet the instructional goals, the size of the computer's hard disk space or file server's hard disk space is critical. Any technology will become extinct and perhaps worthless for instructional purposes. However, several computer models are on the market that have built in "vacancies" for the special purpose of upgrading memory and/or speed of the computer.

EVALUATING HARDWARE COMPONENTS

In addition to the basic computer system components (monitor, CPU, keyboard, mouse, and printer), other components are becoming popular in the business world today. These components include CD-ROM drives, internal facsimiles, and internal modems. If these components are to be used, a plan should be developed to incorporate the technologies into the learning activities.

However, such analysis will be minimal or not necessary if an institution cannot obtain the technology. If the students' use of the extra technology will be limited, teachers should determine whether the components' inclusion is necessary.

CD-ROM. The extensive storage capacity of compact disks for both visual and informational data has made CD-ROMs useful in the business world, and very popular in classrooms. Access to an encyclopedia on a CD could be an asset in any classroom. At this point in the development of CD-ROM (compact disc—read only memory) technology, it would be impractical to add CD-ROM drives to every computer in a classroom, but a special CD-ROM system can be added to a computer network, allowing all users to it. If a school does not have a computer network, one centrally-located computer could be used as the "library" computer.

When evaluating this hardware component, business educators should consider how this component will be incorporated into learning activities to determine whether the use of the CD-ROM justifies its cost.

Fax/modem. As educational institutions become computerized, some school systems have incorporated activities that allow students to share information at various schools via telecommunications. Modems facilitate this capability by connecting computers through telephone lines. Several computer systems are manufactured with internal modems. As instructional aids, facsimile and modem components may not have as great a priority as other equipment. The teacher's role is to determine learning goals and objectives that will help the evaluation process when deciding whether to incorporate these elements.

Laser printers vs. impact printers. The major determinant of the type of printer purchased is usually the cost of the product. In addition to determining what is affordable, the types of documents printed by the students should also be reviewed. Considering the final disposition of most student-generated documents (the wastepaper or recycling basket), purchasing laser printers seems impractical to most business educators. Normal business correspondence (letters, memos, etc.) is acceptable when printed on a 300 dpi (dots per inch) printer. However, 600 dpi creates a much more attractive document when graphics are used. Most educational computer labs should have at least one printer that will print graphics and text at an acceptable quality. Due to the initial expense of purchasing laser printers, educators should consider evaluating ink jet or bubble jet printers for special print jobs.

Ink jet or bubble jet printers that provide a near-laser quality print are becoming widely used in homes and small business offices. These printers are smaller, sometimes portable, and cost a great deal less than laser printers. Although at this point, the cost to print a page with an ink jet and bubble jet printer is more than with a laser printer. If time is a factor, ink jet and bubble jet printers can print only two or three pages a minute as compared to eight pages per minute on a laser printer.

Another factor to consider when evaluating printers for instructional use is the printer's amount of memory. Printers also have RAM (random access memory). When a print job is sent to the printer from the computer, the document is stored in the printer's memory, thereby leaving the computer free to process other documents while waiting for the print job to be completed. The minimum RAM suggested for printers is 2 MB if graphics are involved. Less space (1 MB) would be required for standard text and more space (up to 4 MB) would be suggested for heavy-duty graphics. Although cost is usually the most significant factor affecting the type of printer chosen, the quality of printed documents needed in the classroom should be considered when evaluating printers.

SOFTWARE CONSIDERATIONS

Software selected for classroom use directly affects the learning environment and course objectives. Before making software decisions, educators should consider their instructional goals and student performance objectives as they relate to the use of software packages. Since software applications are used to develop or implement the learning activities, the software chosen must be consistent with the course goals.

IBM vs. Mac. IBM (or IBM clones) software is used more frequently than Macintosh software in the corporate business world. Regardless of the computer environment chosen, the software and hardware must be compatible. Another consideration regarding the computing environment is the need to teach students to learn how to learn. Students should develop skills to transfer their learning from one computer system to another and feel confident that no matter what kind of computer they use, they will be able to complete projects or activities based on previous learning experiences in the classroom. Some schools may want students to use two different computer platforms. Others may want students to become familiar with a popular graphic user environment such as Windows since many people predict that all future software will run under a graphical environment.

Operating systems. Microsoft DOS (disk operating system) is the most commonly used operating system. DOS 6.2 provides a wide range of utility programs that allow users to modify their hard drives to fit their individual needs. The DOSSHELL program is user friendly; however Microsoft's Windows environment is also considered very user-friendly and used extensively by both education and business. Determining which file manager to use in the classroom greatly depends upon the course objectives and learning activities used to meet those objectives.

The Windows 3.11 operating system is a graphical environment that runs in concert with DOS. Because some of the newer software programs require Windows, many computer manufacturers sell their computer systems with Windows already installed. Because Windows provides a graphical interface, students become used to "pointing and clicking" at the applications (pictures) they wish to open. Although Windows is a user-friendly environment, students will not learn how to manipulate DOS subdirectories or other related functions and may become perplexed when faced with a pure DOS environment in the business world. Windows 95 is a disk operating system in and of itself and does not run under MS-DOS. If Windows 95 is accepted by many users in businesses and schools, MS-DOS will become extinct.

Another disk operating system known as OS/2 resembles Windows to a great extent. Although it is a less expensive file manager, many businesses have hesitated to switch from Windows to OS/2 primarily because it was difficult to understand and took a tremendous amount of hard disk space. Windows was introduced to the market before OS/2 and has since become very widely used. OS/2 Warp, a newer release, has had mixed acceptance in the marketplace at this time. Since most new computers come with a disk operating system already loaded on the hard drive, selecting a disk operating system may be of lesser concern than hardware and applications software.

Application programs. The most common software programs used in business include word processing, spreadsheet, database management, graphing, and desktop publishing. Several popular programs are on the market for each type of program. Evaluating computer software can be a very time-consuming and difficult task. Most experts suggest that educators perform a needs analysis (as discussed earlier in the chapter) to produce a clear understanding of what the software package(s) should be able to do for the user. When evaluating software, hardware requirements should be considered first. Do the computers have enough RAM, hard disk space, and a fast enough processor to run the software? Is the software manufacturer a stable company? Will it be around next year? Does it provide an 800 number or any number to call for technical support? Will the product be upgraded? Klopping and Bolgiano (1990) identify some other factors to consider when selecting software application programs including printing features, compatibility with other software programs, ease of use, documentation, training, cost, vendor support, and possible product upgrades.

New versions vs. old versions of software. Another widely-debated subject among business teachers is the question of whether to upgrade when a new version of a software package becomes available. The following factors should be considered when making this decision:

- Have local businesses upgraded their software? If not, do they plan to upgrade in the near future (or even at all)?

- Does this upgrade contain programming "bugs" that need to be worked out? Or, does it eliminate "bugs" in previous versions? Release 1.0 of any software is likely to have bugs.

- Are there textbooks or instructional materials available for this upgrade?

- Is a price discount available if the software is upgraded now? Is it likely the upgrade price will be effective for only a few months?

- Have computer magazines reviewed the new version positively or negatively?

The answers to these questions can help determine whether to upgrade to a new version of a current software package. If businesses are upgrading their software, classrooms should upgrade theirs also. If no instructional materials are available for the new technology, the teachers should consider how significant the changes are between the old version and the new version. In many cases, teachers can use textbooks designed for previous versions of software without making too many modifications in instruction.

SUMMARY

Today, education is very dependent on technology. Business educators need to ensure their roles as leaders in technology by embracing the new technologies that inundate business and industry today. The process of evaluating technology for instructional use can seem like an overwhelming task; the choices made will affect classrooms for many years.

By determining the goals and objectives of the instruction, the needs of the students, and the competencies desired by employers, the technology selection process can become a unique opportunity and challenge for business educators. By evaluating instructional technology for classroom applications, business and educators can become "resident technological experts" in educational institutions and lead their students in obtaining the knowledge and skills necessary to function in the workplace.

REFERENCES

Berger, C. (1993). Teaching with technology. *HEPC: Higher Education Product Companion*, 3, 3.

Goodman, D. (1994). Working with what you've got. *Inc.: 1994 Guide to Office Technology*, 34-36.

Klopping, I. M., and Bolgiano, C. F. (1990). Effective evaluation of off-the-shelf microcomputer software. *Office Systems Research Journal*, 9, 46-50.

Lambrecht, J. J. (1987). Selecting and utilizing hardware and software for the classroom. *Business Education For a Changing World*, Reston, Virginia: National Business Education Association.

Policies Commission for Business and Economic Education. (1993). This we believe about the role of business education in technology. *Business Education Forum*, 48, 11-12.

CHAPTER 11

Redesigning the Classroom To Reflect Technology's Impact

MARSHA BAYLESS

Stephen F. Austin State University, Nacogdoches, Texas

At one time or another every business educator has sketched the "perfect" business classroom. The perfect room has ergonomic furniture appropriately placed, enough equipment that always works, and enough electrical outlets in convenient locations. Seldom, however, do business educators have the opportunity to turn the "perfect" sketch into reality.

More frequently, teachers have an opportunity to revise or replace different components of the classroom over a period of time. As new technology has changed the way that business and computer classrooms are used, redesigning the classroom for the most effective instructional environment has become increasingly important.

The purpose of this chapter is to discuss a number of issues which relate to technology and redesigning the classroom.

CLASSROOM LAYOUT

Incorporating technology effectively in the classroom requires more than just purchasing computers and placing them in an available room. Teaching environments such as computer classrooms and computer labs as well as accounting, keyboarding, office systems, and general purpose classrooms all require the following considerations as technology is added to those classes.

How many different uses will the room have? In the majority of schools the same rooms must be used for many classes. In examining technology's demand for facilities, the educator must determine all the uses for the room. A room which will have some self-paced activities and some teacher-directed presentations may require a compromise on design. While a cluster or pod arrangement may be desirable for self-paced activities, a more traditional arrangement may work better with large group presentations. The room may also be used for courses which use little or no technology; the design must also facilitate the needs of such groups.

What is the estimated life of the technology with this design? Once the classroom is arranged to meet the current needs of technology, the classroom instructor must envision how technology will impact the design in future years. For example, will adding voice recognition systems make any difference to the classroom layout?

How will current teaching theories and goals affect the classroom design? If teachers plan to incorporate collaborative work in the classroom, the room design may be different than if individualized instruction is used.

A general purpose classroom may require little technology beyond a portable teaching station encompassing a notebook computer, LCD panel, and overhead projector. However, some office systems classrooms may require additional technology such as scanners, fax machines, and modems.

SPECIAL CONSIDERATIONS

When redesigning a classroom, instructors must examine the logistics of the new arrangement in terms of fire and safety codes. One of the safety concerns faced by educators is what to do with all the cords and cables generated by computers and other technology. Selecting furniture with cable troughs to contain the cords, tying cords together off the floor, and arranging furniture to keep cords out of traffic areas are some options which may be used. Cords which must extend across the floor pose safety problems.

The Americans with Disabilities Act (ADA) addresses many issues for Americans who experience physical barriers. As the workplace becomes more available to such students, they will look for training in business and computer classrooms. These classrooms should have furniture which will allow accommodation for persons in wheelchairs, i.e. adjustable desk heights and wider aisles. Extra chairs and space may be needed if an attendant such as a notetaker must accompany a student to class.

COMPUTERS AND PRINTERS

As classrooms vary in both size and shape, the number of computers and printers in the classroom should be based on how the technology is used. Several factors should be considered.

Small number of computers. Classrooms with fewer than 20 computers have several advantages. The most important, perhaps, is that the instructor has an opportunity to help each student more frequently during a class session. Instructors will also have a smaller number of computers to maintain. In addition, by having a smaller number of computers, it may be easier for the instructor to gain the attention of the class.

The primary disadvantage of having a small number of computers occurs when more students want to enroll than the number of computers in the room. No one likes to turn away students but most teachers do not want students to have to "double-up" on computers either. In addition, with a small number of computers, less equipment will be available for backup equipment in case of computer malfunction.

Large number of computers. The biggest advantage of a large classroom is that larger class sizes can be maintained. The instructor will have an opportunity to utilize teaching strategies such as encouraging students to help each other and developing teams of student analysts to diagnose problems. Diagnostic skills and team cooperation skills can be invaluable in the workplace.

The main disadvantage of having a larger number of computers in a room is that the teacher may not be available to help each student quickly. In addition, more computers will require more maintenance. Also, equipment and software upgrades costs may be higher with more machines to upgrade; however, discounts may be available on large orders, providing some cost savings.

Backup computers. As experienced computer classroom teachers know, computers do malfunction. A disadvantage occurs when the class size exactly matches the number of computers available. Having backup computers can be extremely important.

An alternative for the instructor with no backup equipment is to always have at least a portion of the assignment that can be done with partners so that a student with a disabled machine can be "partnered" with another student. One example is a "partners-across-the-room strategy." At the beginning of the term, partners are assigned in different parts of the room. If a computer or printer breaks down, the partners get together to share the functional machine. This type of approach not only allows all students to work on assignments but can reduce the sense of computer ownership that some students develop.

Number and type of printers. The number and type of printers depend on several factors. A decision should be made about whether dot matrix or laser printers should be used. The type of work the students are completing could be an important factor in this choice. For those labs that intend to focus on graphics and desktop publishing applications, laser printers with added memory are critical. In addition, graphic intensive applications require more time to print. If the purpose of the lab is primarily word processing, spreadsheet, and database applications, dot matrix printers may be sufficient.

Other factors such as volume of usage and cost must be considered. Laser printers are more expensive to operate than dot matrix printers; laser printers require expensive toner and cut sheet paper. Color printers (dot matrix, ink jet, and laser) are becoming more affordable but may require supplies that are too costly for the average business classroom. In addition, having several types of printers requires keeping supplies on hand for all printers.

Another factor to consider before selecting the appropriate number of printers is how the work is to be printed. If an entire class of 25 students is expected to print their work at the end of the class period, chaos can ensue if only one printer is available. If students work on a self-paced level and print throughout the class period, an end-of-the period dilemma may not occur. As both students and teachers can be frustrated by problems with printing, allotting some of the equipment assets in this area will certainly be worthwhile. Another factor to consider when selecting printers is the ultimate use or disposal of the printout.

Generally, one dot-matrix printer is needed for every four to eight computers. However, with high volume or graphics-intensive printing, two to four computers per dot matrix printer may be a better choice. The guidelines for a laser printer would be based on both the speed of the printer and the volume and intensity of usage. In low-usage situations, one laser printer for 15 computers would be acceptable. In high usage situations (especially those with graphics), one laser printer with expanded memory for each 8-10 computers would be a better choice.

OTHER TECHNOLOGY CONSIDERATIONS

Computers and printers are frequently joined by other types of technology, which may affect how the classroom facilities are arranged.

Local area networks. The design of the network may help to determine how many stations should be grouped together. Checking the manual of the network software or visiting with a local area network administrator will be critical in the classroom layout. With an IBM Token Ring, the teacher should check to see how many computers can be attached to each multiple access unit (MAU) and decide where the MAUs will be placed. If 8-port MAUs are being purchased, a teacher may want to plan on having eight computers in a pod or row. If 12-port MAUs are used, that could impact the arrangement of computers.

Before installing an Ethernet network, instructors should check to see how many computers can be attached to each hub. The location of the MAUs or hubs should be considered. If many computers are on a network or if several networks are connected to a backbone network, the school should plan to put in a wiring closet that can be locked.

Space should be allowed for the network file server. The network file server is a computer dedicated to maintaining the network. For this reason, it should not be counted as a student work station. In fact, if the network file server must be located in the classroom, it should be placed away from computers the students are using. An ideal location for the network file server would be in a separate office easily accessed by the network administrator. If an instructor also serves as the network administrator, access away from the classroom would allow system maintenance at any time. If the network file server is located in the classroom, security codes and levels of access should be used so that no one inadvertently changes information that would affect the network operation.

Connectivity. The teacher should be able to demonstrate such things as electronic mail in the classroom. An ideal situation would be to have connectivity for all students at their computers through the network. If the network is connected to a larger network that has access to the Internet, students can utilize that communication tool. Another option would be for the instructor to have a modem (either internal or external) and a telephone jack in the classroom so that connectivity could be demonstrated.

Portable telephone. As computer and software maintenance becomes increasingly driven by phone calls to helpdesks, a cordless telephone is a valuable option for an instructor. When the telephone connection is not in the classroom, but in a nearby office, a cordless telephone enables the instructor to take the phone right to the machine exhibiting difficulty.

Storage. The classroom design should include storage cupboards or cabinets to accommodate student diskettes as well as other items which may not be used for every class period, such as scanners, computer software programs, and documentation.

TYPES OF COMPUTER CLASSROOMS AND LABS

Computer classrooms can be used in a variety of ways. While at times they may be used for large group instruction, they may also be used for individual work or may serve as open labs for students to complete projects.

Clustered work stations. Work stations may be clustered into groups or pods as shown in Lab Design A. Such a design would be the best choice for a room which is primarily used for intensive computer work. This design allows six students to share one printer. Computer cables are safely stored out of walkways with this design. The design provides several locations for wheel chair access because of the space which is available. An added advantage to this design is that students can easily be divided into teams of three. They can complete collaborative work as well as assist each other if they encounter problems while the instructor is engaged in another part of the room. The location of the printers makes it easy for the instructor to maintain them without disrupting student work.

If a teacher uses the rear wall or front wall for projection of computer demonstrations, all students may be able to see the presentation by turning to the side. The main disadvantage to this classroom arrangement is that it is more difficult for the instructor to assess the progress of the class as a whole.

For security sake, the file server should be in a separate office and not in the main classroom. This office should be large enough to store various

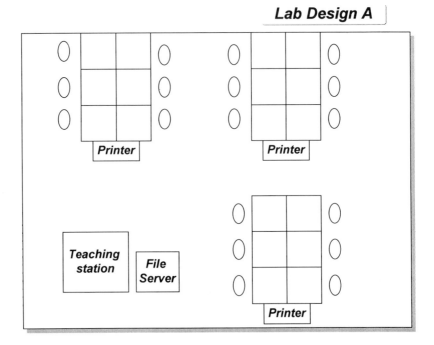

Lab Design A

backup equipment, the teaching station when it is not in use, and, possibly, the wiring closet for a computer network. If windows are placed between the office and the classroom, instructors can work at the file server computer and still view the classroom.

Multipurpose classroom. A more traditional class arrangement can be seen in Lab Design B. This classroom could be a multipurpose room where computers are not used extensively. If the room is used for general classes that do not use computers, the school may wish to invest in devices that will move keyboards and mice out of the way so they can be protected from damage. Such steps will also provide more desktop space for noncomputer students. The main advantage of this classroom design is that all students face the instructor. If teacher demonstrations are frequent, this design would be very effective.

When using this classroom design, teams of four could be organized to help each other. The two students closest to the printer could be responsible for loading paper and seeing that the printer is on-line. The two outside students could be diagnosticians so that if anyone in the row has a difficulty, they can analyze the problem and provide assistance.

Another advantage of this design is that after students begin working on the computers, the instructor can, from the back of the classroom, look across the room to see if students are having difficulties. With this design, more printers per computer are available than in Lab Design A. This lab may be

Lab Design B

Teaching Station

File Server

P

P

P

P

P

P

P = Printer

effective for a heavy volume of documents that must be completed at about the same time, such as end-of-class graphic printouts.

In a multipurpose room, security of the file server and portable computers is even more of a concern because teachers may not know that no one should use the file server who is not a knowledgeable network administrator; hence, the need for a separate office to house the file server is even greater than in a computer lab.

Teaching station. All computer classrooms should include a complete teaching station that is on a moveable cart. If the teaching station is portable, the instructor can move the station to a traditional classroom to demonstrate activities that students will be doing in the lab during the next class period, thereby maximizing the students' time when they are in the computer classroom.

The portable station should consist of a computer (preferably a notebook), an LCD panel, and a high density overhead projector or any other equipment that allows projection of images from a computer. The demonstration computer should have a large enough hard drive so that various instructors can install single copies of software on it for demonstration purposes. Additionally, the computer should include an internal modem so the instructor can demonstrate connectivity. In fact, the capabilities of this computer should exceed those of any other system in the classroom lab, although it could be used as a backup student work station.

To use a teaching station effectively, the classroom should have a projection screen or wall surface (such as a white market board) that can be used for projection. Another option would be to use a large screen monitor and appropriate hardware to project the computer screen upon the monitor.

Computer lab. In a computer lab, students are expected to work independently without close teacher supervision. An instructor may assign projects that are to be finished by the student in the computer lab. Postsecondary institutions are more likely than secondary schools to use a lab. Software in a computer lab should be easy to use. Textbooks should be tutorial books that provide step-by-step instructions. On-line tutorials can be very useful also.

Computer labs are often larger than classroom labs, sometimes having 50-70 computers in them. The design of the lab should lend itself to individualized instruction as much as possible. Some computer labs have stations along all the outside walls of the classroom with printers and work tables located in the middle of the room. Other labs may have arrangements similar to individual study carrels in a library. A lab director or assistant must be available during the hours a lab is open including at night. A lab director and lab assistants perform the following duties:

- Assisting students with a variety of software programs
- Providing security of hardware and software
- Assisting students with printer problems.

A lab director may find it difficult to find assistants who know every possible software package that instructors want to use. In fact, a school may need to have teachers select one word processing, spreadsheet, and database software program to be used in the lab; otherwise, three different teachers may want to use three different word processing programs.

Every computer classroom/lab should be concerned with virus control and prevention. Each standalone computer or computer network should have virus protection software installed in such a way that it automatically scans for viruses on hard disk drives. Additionally, lab assistants may want to implement a policy of scanning students' floppy disks before they are used in the lab.

CLASSROOM FURNITURE AND THE ENVIRONMENT

Ergonomic factors are important considerations when choosing furniture for the classroom. Musculoskeletal injuries are skyrocketing in the workplace. Such problems as repetitive stress injuries and lower back pain are increasing the health costs of American business. Estimates of the annual cost to business of repetitive stress injuries is nearly $20 billion (Wolkimir, 1994). An environment which closely matches people, function, and furnishings will also provide the best atmosphere for learning. Factors such as adjustability, frequent changes of position, and work design should be considered in furniture selection (Allie, 1994).

Future business workers can be better prepared by enforcing these elements in the classroom:

1. Schedule periodic 10 to 30-second breaks for change of movement and activities such as hand exercises or stretching.

2. Adjust seating and the slant of the computer so that wrists are tilting downward or are at least flat.

3. Direct students to have their torsos in a forward-tilt position with back support.

4. Do not enforce rigid posture requirements.

Student desks. The suggested height for a nonkeyboard work surface is 28-32 inches. However, the recommended height for a keyboard is lower with a range of 23-28 inches. The depth of the work surface should vary to accommodate the tasks and equipment used. The minimum leg space width is 24-30 inches. These standards have been established by the American National Standards Institute (Joyce and Wallersteiner, 1989).

Adjustable computer furniture is an excellent idea. In reality, however, a desk with a computer is difficult to adjust. Adjusting the height of all furniture in a pod may be a more practical idea. Then shorter students can be seated in one pod and taller students in another pod. Foot rests are another option for shorter students.

Computer desks should be designed to accommodate the necessary cables. Desks with built-in cable troughs and electrical outlets are preferable, but desks with an overhang can provide space for cables to be anchored under the overhang.

Chairs. Adjustable chairs are the best way to accommodate all heights of students. The ideal chair has adjustable pneumatic lift, five castor wheels, and lumbar support. With such chairs, students can be taught quickly how to adjust them. Chairs that require extensive effort to be adjusted, such as loosening and adjusting of bolts, are not useful in a room with several classes of students each day.

Lighting. Classroom lighting can affect performance on the computer. Windows can provide natural sunlight, but sunlight can also cause glare on some computer screens. Furthermore, overhead fluorescent lights can cause glare. Task lighting, blinds to reduce outdoor light, careful placement of monitors, and glare reducing devices are some ways to reduce eye strain. Instructors should be aware that classrooms with perfect lighting in the morning may have glare problems in the afternoon.

Noise. Noise can be a problem in a computer classroom because of printers and multimedia systems with sound boards. Several steps can be taken to reduce noise levels. Carpeting can be used to absorb sound, and static-resistant carpet can reduce static electricity in a computer room, as long as the carpet is not shampooed. Fabric wall panels can be used to reduce noise.

Dot matrix printers are the noisiest items in classrooms. However, acoustic sound hoods are available to mute printer noise. While more costly, laser printers are much quieter than dot matrix printers.

Multimedia systems with sound boards and video/sound clips can increase the level of noise in classrooms. Classrooms can be equipped with headphones for each computer so that multimedia software can be heard only by the operator at each computer.

Electrical, heating, and cooling needs. As more traditional classrooms install computers, increased electrical usage should be a consideration. Newer computers and printers require more power than older equipment such as calculators. Electricians should be consulted before making a major computer upgrade in a classroom.

Each computer room should have individual thermostats if not separate heating and air conditioning systems. Computers generate a great amount of heat, making a computer lab very uncomfortable for students unless a teacher has direct control over the heating and cooling system. Computer circuitry is very sensitive to extremely high or low temperatures, which means that a constant temperature should be maintained. If temperatures are below 50 degrees in a classroom, computers should not be turned on until the temperature is raised.

Clean environment. A clean environment helps keep printers, disk drives, and other computer components in good working condition. Traditional chalkboards should not be used in computer rooms because of chalk dust. White marker boards are preferable, and they can serve as projection screens. Monitors and computers should be cleaned weekly. In fact, students can be delegated tasks such as cleaning marker boards, monitors, and computers.

CLASSROOM SECURITY

Security practices and procedures should be implemented in every school/classroom that contains computer equipment. Open labs with minimal supervision require more security than supervised computer classrooms. To secure equipment, cable locks or bolts can be used to attach computer equipment to desks.

Computer classrooms should not have outside windows and should not be close to outside exit doors. If classrooms have windows, they should be long and narrow and the type that cannot be opened. If a classroom has windows, the windows should have blinds and the blinds should be closed each evening. Dead bolt locks on computer classrooms can be an extra security measure. However, a separate alarm system for each computer classroom is more effective than dead bolt locks.

Other security problems include tampering with software, hardware, and/or networks. Passwords and other security devices should be used to limit access to sensitive computer programs. Students who use computer networks should only be allowed access to software that they use in their classes.

Original copies of software should be locked securely in cabinets. The only copies used in classrooms should be backup copies. This way a clean copy of the software is available if backup copies become infected by viruses or if they are inadvertently deleted.

Computer viruses can cause havoc in a computer classroom. All computer disks brought into a classroom should be scanned for viruses before they are used. Viruses can cause damage to files on floppy disks and hard disks if they are not found quickly and eliminated. Since new viruses are developed almost daily, new virus detection programs should be purchased at least each year or two.

A MASTER PLAN FOR CLASSROOM REDESIGN

An analysis of the current classroom facilities should be conducted before a plan for updating a classroom is designed. The Facilities Plan Guide should be used to determine the important components of a master plan for classroom redesign. A master plan may be based on immediate renovation or it may take three to five years to accomplish. Instructors and administrators should have input in the development of a master plan for classroom redesign.

FACILITIES PLAN GUIDE

Analyze the classroom to determine each of these factors.

Priority	Year for Change
1 = Highest Priority	1 = Year One
2 = Priority	2 = Year Two
3 = Low Priority	3 = Year Three
4 = No change needed	

Area	Priority	Year
Requirements of Americans with Disabilities Act	_____	_____
Safety concerns (cables, etc.)	_____	_____
Computers	_____	_____
Printers	_____	_____
Local area network	_____	_____
Connectivity (electronic mail, etc.)	_____	_____
Portable telephone	_____	_____
Storage (for disks, software, scanners, etc.)	_____	_____
Arrangement of equipment and furniture	_____	_____

Teaching station (portable)   _____   _____
Computer desks, tables (adjustable)   _____   _____
Chairs, ergonomic (adjustable)   _____   _____
Lighting   _____   _____
Noise   _____   _____
Electricity and power requirements   _____   _____
Clean environment (dust free, white marker boards)   _____   _____
Security (hardware, software, virus protection)   _____   _____
Comments:

SUMMARY

As with any successful classroom, the environment of the room requires careful planning and design. Careful consideration of issues such as equipment selection, furniture choice, room arrangement, and task design can help provide an ergonomic environment for students now and in the future.

REFERENCES

Allie, P. F. (1994). Ergonomics and the healthy office. *Managing Office Technology, 39*(10), 31-32.

Joyce, M., & Wallersteiner, U. (1989). *Ergonomics humanizing the automated office.* Cincinnati, OH: South-Western Publishing Company.

Wolkomir, R. (1994). When the work you do ends up costing you an arm and a leg. *Smithsonian, 25*(3), 90-101.

CHAPTER 12

Computer Operating Systems and Graphical User Environments—The State of the Art

TERRY D. LUNDGREN

Eastern Illinois University, Charleston, Illinois

Personal computers continue to expand their influence in business and education in ways that were not imagined 10 years ago. In the early 1980s, computer usage was restricted to the corporate mainframe and its select group of operators, programmers, and systems analysts in the data processing shop. The user of computer data was isolated very effectively from the hardware and software by a layer of data processing staff. User requests for data took weeks and even months to be filled.

A similar situation existed in academia. Most universities had acquired mainframes by the early 1980s for administrative and research activities. Computer usage was controlled by the computing staff. Instructional use of computers was limited to programming classes and an occasional research project requiring statistical analysis. The student using the mainframe computer system faced an interface that, in the kindest words, could be called "user hostile."

Personal computers (PCs) have changed all of this. Though mainframes still exist and continue their role with little change in the interface, personal computers have burst upon the scene with user friendliness. Schools have embraced the technology, and the use of computer applications increases every year in virtually every academic area. The personal computer allows for hands-on use in an atmosphere that encourages computer literacy. The increased use of the personal computer has driven applications interfaces to become friendlier. Personal computer operating systems have developed a much friendlier interface with the user, and that interface extends to applications software also.

OPERATING SYSTEMS OVERVIEW

Although each computer application could provide a unique interface, there are many advantages if the operating system defines the basic user interface. To see how this system would be accomplished, begin by looking at the characteristics of an operating system, then examine the types of user interfaces, and follow with some notes on the transferability of skills across types of user interfaces.

Operating system (OS) characteristics. Operating systems are programs that control the input, processing, and output functions of a computer. The most common operating systems for personal computers are MS-DOS, OS/2,

Macintosh operating system, and UNIX. The role of the operating system is to provide a control program that can manage the hardware and coordinate the execution of application programs. Additionally, the operating system provides a method that allows users to perform certain file and disk functions such as deleting a file or formatting a disk. In most cases, only one OS program can be running on your computer; the UNIX operating system is the exception, allowing MS-DOS and Macintosh operating systems to run under the UNIX system.

The operating system is tied to the hardware, particularly the microprocessor; in fact, operating systems are designed for specific categories of microprocessors. Today Macintosh computers use one operating system, and IBM compatible computers use a different operating system. Some operating systems are designed for a certain class and speed of microprocessor. For example, an operating system may be designed for use on a computer with a very fast 486 or Pentium chip, e.g. 486DX2/66Mhz or Pentium/60 Mhz.

Multitasking is one of the most important functions of the two newest operating systems—OS/2 Warp and Windows 95. Multitasking means that more than one application can be operating concurrently; for example, a user can see on a monitor a spreadsheet created with Lotus 1-2-3 and also a report created with Microsoft Word. Multitasking can be effective in varying degrees, depending on the computer hardware. Even though the ability to multitask means an OS requires a very fast microprocessor and a lot of RAM memory, the trend is toward multitasking operating systems.

Most contemporary operating systems use virtual memory. On PC's, the OS can take advantage of the 386 and higher microprocessor's virtual mode and effectively create multiple virtual machines. Virtual memory allows computers to run as if they have more memory than what they really have. If there is not enough system memory for a particular application, the OS will use some of the hard disk to simulate system memory. This ability to use all memory resources can significantly increase the abilities of a computer system (Lundgren and Garrett, 1994).

User interface. The user interface is the way that the computer operator actually performs input and output (I/O) on a system. There are two different types of interface—the command line and the graphical user interface (GUI).

Most mainframe, mini, and personal computer DOS operating systems have a command line interface. This interface requires the user to key in the proper commands to carry out the OS function desired. The user keys in the command line in response to a screen prompt. The command line will always consist of the command and several parameters separated from each other by a delimiter or separator. One example of a command line is dir a:/p. That command allows the user to view the first page of a directory (list) of file names stored on Drive A of a computer system. For knowledgeable users, the command line is fast and efficient; but for new users, it is an obscure, difficult-to-understand system.

The graphical user interface, also known as a GUI (pronounced "gooey" or "gooie"), is not new. GUI applications were first developed for a Xerox Star computer in the early 1980s. More recently, GUI applications have become a standard feature on Apple Macintosh computers. Most GUI applications use a mouse to point at icons (pictures on the screen) to perform operations. For example, an icon of a trash can could represent a delete/erase operation. An icon of a file folder with an arrow pointing into the folder could represent saving a file to disk. GUI interfaces also use dialog boxes that contain messages and/or ask questions of the user.

Generally, GUI interfaces use a mouse rather than the keyboard for command input. Instead of entering a command, a mouse moves a pointer on the display screen to point to icons that represent the desired activity. Basic mouse operations are essential to using a GUI system; these operations include pointing, clicking, double clicking, and clicking and dragging. Operations are selected from the desktop by moving the mouse pointer to point to a menu item, a button, or an icon and then performing the mouse operation.

With a graphical user interface, the screen is viewed as a desktop and windows can be opened to run different applications and perform operations. Proponents of the GUI say that it is more intuitive and that new users can more quickly learn the basic skills. GUI users may be more creative in their output than DOS command line users. On the other hand, DOS command line users may be more productive in terms of output. In any case, a GUI interface does not replace the keyboard as a data entry device, but it does replace keying command line entries manually.

CURRENT OPERATING SYSTEMS & GRAPHICAL USER ENVIRONMENTS

A wide range of personal computer operating systems is available ranging from DOS versions to UNIX, Macintosh OS/2, System 7, and others. This section reviews the major operating systems for personal computers in order of their installed base. Each OS contains a brief description, idiosyncracies, and notes on performance.

The actual use of an operating system remains an estimate because multiple operating systems can be on one computer or computer network. The installed base concept relies on the number of units sold, which is an admittedly rough estimate of actual use. Taking into account the applications designed and sold for a specific operating system helps refine the installed base figures.

DOS. This system is the most popular for personal computers, with an estimated 50 percent of the personal computer market. DOS was originally designed for the IBM PC, and today many personal computers use a version of this system. DOS versions began with 1.0 and have been followed with 1.1 to 6.2, with more versions coming in the future. This is a decimal numbering system, and the numbers to the left of the decimal indicate major versions whereas the numbers after the decimal indicate minor revisions. In addition to Microsoft's MS-DOS, other DOS software includes IBM's PC-DOS, Novell's DOS, and Zenith DOS. The majority of the market share is clearly held by MS-DOS.

The current versions of MS-DOS 6.2, Novell DOS 7.0, and IBM's PC-DOS 6.1 are all comparably priced and offer similar features. They contain memory management, file compression, antivirus protection, backup, and other utilities (Wolverton, 1994). New versions are released about every 18 months. DOS has evolved into a complex and powerful operating system. To fully appreciate and use all its capabilities takes considerable study and experience (Goodman and Soucha, 1993).

Windows. Microsoft's Windows 3.0 was named the most successful new product of 1990, a year in which more than a million copies were sold. Windows was the first successful GUI for the PC family, and it has had a tremendous impact. Version 3.1 was released in 1992, with Windows 4.0, now called Windows 95, expected in 1995 (Bott, 1994). About 20 million copies of 3.1 have been sold and an estimated 1 million copies are sold every month (Leyenberger, 1993). Recent additions to the Windows line are Windows NT (New Technology) and Windows for WorkGroups. These variants include networking capabilities and 32 bit operations.

Virtually all major applications programs have Windows versions such as WordPerfect for Windows and Lotus 1-2-3 for Windows. A major advantage is that applications written for Windows use the **CUA** (Common User Access), which is Microsoft's standard for terminology, commands, and keystrokes. CUA makes applications easier to learn and to use since the user interface is standard; it increases the transferability of skills for different applications for the user.

With the ability to run thousands of existing applications as well as Windows versions of almost all the popular applications, it is easy to see why so many users are adopting Windows. Industry experts predict that the product's popularity will grow in the 1990s, with many of the largest businesses adopting the package. Though difficult to estimate, Windows and its variants probably account for about one-third of the OS market today.

The term operating environment was introduced with Windows because it runs under DOS; that is, DOS must be running for Windows to operate. Although this fact might seem like an important distinction, it is not. For the user, the practical implication is that both DOS and Windows must be purchased for a system. Windows NT and Windows 95 are complete operating systems.

One well-publicized feature of Windows is **OLE** (Object Linking and Embedding). OLE allows the user to include data from another program in a document. Windows 3.0 has **DDE** (Dynamic Data Exchange), which stores the data in the document with links to the original so that if the original is changed, so is the data in the linked document. OLE goes a bit further and puts only the pointer in the document instead of a copy of the data. Either the original document or the pointer can be used to edit the data.

Both DDE and OLE require the cooperation of the application programs. For example, a spreadsheet created with Lotus 1-2-3 for Windows could be cut and pasted (dynamically) into a report created with Lotus' Ami Pro word processor. If the spreadsheet needed to be changed, it could be accessed by retrieving the spreadsheet file or by clicking on the spreadsheet pointer within the Ami Pro document. Then, any change made in the spreadsheet would be made in both locations—in the spreadsheet file itself and in the report created with word processing.

Windows NT is a complete 32-bit operating system that does not need DOS to run. It is designed to run on at least a 486 MPU with lots of RAM (8MB, 16MB, 32MB, or more), a high resolution monitor, and a hard disk with at least 200MB capacity. It will compete directly with IBM's OS/2. It is designed for multitasking and multiprocessing and can make efficient use of all the memory stored in the system.

IBM's OS/2. Though available for some years, IBM's OS/2 did not become commercially viable until version 2.0 was introduced in early 1992. OS/2 is a GUI multitasking 32-bit operating system. Its claim was that it was a "better DOS than DOS" and a "better Windows than Windows" (Salemi, 1992). OS/2 can completely replace both DOS and Windows while running almost all of their applications as well as applications written for it. The GUI is quite different from Windows, but not difficult to learn.

The latest version is OS/2 2.1 and OS/2 for Windows. The installed base is 4.5 million (Black, 1994). If IBM continues to back OS/2, it may become a viable alternative OS. Because only IBM offers OS/2 bundled with their hardware, getting it on any other type of PC will involve an upgrade installation. OS/2 requires a tremendous amount of hard disk space.

OS/2 has earned a reputation for difficulty in installation, inability to run many popular DOS and Windows programs, and slow speed (Langa, 1994). Adoption of OS/2 and OS/2 Warp has been hindered because not a lot of applications programs have been rewritten to run under OS/2. IBM is a major player in the OS arena, and its support is a long-term guarantee of its survival in the short term.

Apple's System 7. Presently, the Apple Macintosh or Mac includes the System 7 operating system software with its computer. The System 7 OS represents a long line of evolution from the first practical GUI to a really complete package today. This software is a proprietary OS based on a proprietary microprocessor. There are no legal OS variants, only versions of Apple's. Although Apple is estimated to have about 10-15 percent of the personal computer market, the proprietary nature of its products has restricted the amount of press and information.

Apples are quite popular in educational settings because of a generous educational marketing policy, but they have only a small share of computers in the business world. Macs are used in business as executive workstations, for CAD/CAM applications, desktop publishing (DTP), and other applications that require layout and graphic capabilities. They are popular in advertising departments and newspaper businesses. However, there is a clear trend toward using PC-based systems rather than Macs in desktop publishing and the graphics area (Seymour, 1994).

Other operating systems. The three previously mentioned PC operating systems and the Mac's proprietary operating system completely dominate the personal computer market, but a number of other operating systems are available and some older systems are still in use.

- Uncommon GUI's, such as Digital Research's GEM and others, are used in a number of products.

- The UNIX versions for personal computers, such as Chorus/MiX and UNIX-Ware, are derived from the UNIX versions used on multiple user mainframe systems.

- CP/M and its variants are still available for personal computer. This Control Program for Personal computers was very popular in the 1980's; the main versions were from Digital Research.

- Multiple personality OS's that run applications designed for two more other operating systems, such as SoftPC (Mac and UNIX), Wabi (UNIX and Windows 3.1), and PC-Xware (UNIX and Windows) are also available.

- Pen-based operating systems that accept handwritten input using a special pen are hybrid GUI's combining OCR with GUI's, e.g. Digital Research's GEOWorks variant used in the CASIO Zoomer and Apple's Newton PDA's.

SELECTING AN OPERATING SYSTEM

When selecting an operating system from a pedagogical perspective, a number of factors should be considered. The broad goal is to provide students with the exposure and skills that will enable them to compete effectively in the job market. Therefore, we need to provide students with current OS expertise as well as knowledge about future operating systems. This section examines specific operating system selection issues in the context of those educational goals.

Selection constraints. The most important constraint is the fact that it is not usually feasible to specify an OS when a system is purchased. For example, any PC that is purchased today will be pre-loaded with DOS 6.x and Windows 3.x. A different choice may mean that the bundled software will have to be discarded and additional money spent for an alternative operating system. There are exceptions; for example, many of the IBM systems can be selected with either their version of DOS or OS/2. The advantage of accepting the bundled OS is that the user can be reasonably certain of getting the most popular OS at the time.

For older computers that need an OS upgrade, there are additional constraints. Like applications software, operating systems have grown continually in complexity and size and now require more RAM memory and more hard disk space. The question of whether to upgrade the operating system should be evaluated in terms of providing students with the broadest educational opportunities.

Hardware requirements. DOS makes the least demand on the system hardware. DOS will still run on any compatible PC with any configuration of memory and disk storage. The general rule is to upgrade immediately to the latest version of DOS, but before upgrading multiple computers, one computer should be used as a test vehicle to make sure that the proposed upgrade is feasible.

Use of a GUI like Windows 3.x or OS/2 will require substantial system hardware resources. The GUI is graphical, and graphical applications demand high resolution color displays and additional memory. Minimal requirements for a GUI are a VGA monitor, a hard disk, a pointing device such as a mouse, and 4 MB RAM. The hard disk capacity must be adequate for a GUI operating system. For example, Windows needs a hard disk with 6 to 10 MB of free space. For practical purposes, this means that a 40 MB hard disk should be considered a minimum.

Transferability of skills. Do students need experience in all possible types of operating systems? Or is there sufficient transferability of skills so that extensive experience with one OS will be sufficient? There are no easy answers to those questions. Since all operating systems are very similar in terms of the functions that they provide, the student should gain extensive experience with one modern OS in order to appreciate the capabilities involved. Considerable emphasis should be placed on the functions from a conceptual perspective with continual reminders that the student is using one feature of a particular OS.

Learning a new operating system interface is neither intuitive nor obvious. Learning the command lines used with MS-DOS is not a skill that will transfer to a GUI operating system such as Windows. In fact, learning System 7 on a Mac will not transfer particularly well to OS/2 nor Windows. However, learning to use the mouse to select icons and menus is a transferrable skill. Educators should use the installed base of operating systems in business as a guide. Since PCs outnumber Macintoshes almost ten to one in businesses, students should at least become skilled with a current version of an operating system for the PC—DOS, Windows, or OS/2.

OPERATING SYSTEM TRENDS

New operating systems include more functions than basic input/output, memory management, and utilities. Today, operating systems often include:

- Applets or little applications consisting of a scheduler, notepads, calculator, clock, cardfile, editor, and others

- Virus protection that can check a system and disk for a virus infection and constantly guard against infection

- Recovery programs that allow undeletion of files and unformatting of a disk

- File compression that allows files to be transparently compressed and uncompressed, effectively increasing disk space

- Customization of the commands, their use, and the output that results including display and keyboard control.

These features are in addition to more sophisticated memory management and optimization features. The above features are meant to be employed by the knowledgeable user. In addition to the increasing inclusion of functions into the OS, other trends are emerging.

OS trends. Some new OS features are "leaked" to computer publications by software manufacturers. Sometimes these turn out to be vaporware and never actually materialize. However, the following ones have considerable validity and are likely to occur and become commercially viable:

- The Taligent operating system (code name Pink) from partners IBM and Apple is designed for the PowerPC microprocessor unit. It will be a GUI system based on a proprietary microprocessor said to be equivalent to the Intel Pentium 66MHz, but costing much less.

- On the market now is a Mac Quadra 610 equipped with a hardware board containing a 486SX/25MHz microprocessor that will run DOS 6.2. It is touted as a boon for training and education where tight budgets require doubling up (Thompson, 1994).

- Operating systems that will support SMP (symmetric multiprocessing) are expected in the future. SMP systems that use multiple microprocessors include

Windows NT and OS/2 Release 2.2. The implications of being able to use two or more Intel Pentium 66MHz chips on a desktop unit are staggering.

- Operating systems that will support voice input are also a trend. Microsoft has a sound module in Windows 95, and Apple Computer's System 7.5 upgrade claims voice-synthesis and PlainTalk voice-recognition capabilities.

These trends not only suggest that operating systems are evolving at a rapid rate but also indicate that educators should be cautious about operating system instruction. Teaching students all the intricacies of MS-DOS 6.2 because it has the largest installed base may not serve students well when students graduate two, three, or four years later and use a new GUI operating system.

Therefore, the best strategy for educators is to emphasize the concepts of the OS and to minimize detailed hands-on skills. At the present time, students should experience both a command line system and a graphical user interface. Schools should continue to upgrade OS's as businesses adopt new operating systems. To introduce new operating systems, teachers should obtain demonstration disks of the latest OS's. Emphasis should be placed on the features of operating systems rather than the skills needed on a specific operating system.

OS sales projections. The following table of new unit projections (in millions) shows that the GUI OS is expected to increase its market in the next few years (Foley, 1994).

	1993	1994	1995	1996	1997
DOS (MS, Novell, NEC, and IBM)	16.0	10.4	7.0	2.2	0.6
Windows	24.4	34.4	40.1	44.2	51.3
Windows NT	0.3	1.0	2.7	7.1	11.3
Mac	3.6	4.6	5.8	6.6	7.2
OS/2	1.0	1.1	1.2	1.4	1.5
Other (UNIX, Taligent, etc.)	1.5	1.6	1.8	2.1	2.7

Notice that all the GUI OS's steadily increase while the command line DOS systems steadily decrease.

Virtual reality OS interface. The primary changes in OS interfaces have been in user friendliness. To be user friendly, an operating system has to be designed so that a computer operator can use most of its features without ever opening a book or taking a class. While the movement away from the command line and to a graphical user interface is an improvement in user friendliness, new operating systems are likely to move to a virtual world or virtual reality interface (Kantrowitz, 1994).

A number of software companies have leaked information about this new OS interface. Microsoft's code name for their version of a virtual world interface is "Utopia." It uses a mouse similar to a GUI, but the icons and desktop display are replaced by pictures of the physical world.

Utopia's opening screen is a picture of an office showing the desk, windows, doors, file cabinets, waste basket, a desk calendar, phone, pen, and so on. To write a letter, the user clicks on the pen. To retrieve a stored letter, the user clicks on a file cabinet drawer, which opens and displays the file folders. To conduct a banking transaction, the user clicks on the office door, and the screen changes to the building lobby with the appropriate display. In the lobby, the user can click on the outside doors, and the screen changes to the street with buildings, including a bank. A click on the bank building, and the screen displays the inside of the bank. The user can then select the bank transaction desired.

If this new virtual interface does become a well-accepted operating system, it is likely to be at a time in the future when computers are used more widely in homes and elementary schools. By the time those users become postsecondary students, teaching the operating system interface will not be required!

REFERENCES

Allen, D. (February, 1994). Beyond the GUI. *BYTE.* 19:10.

Black, E. (January, 1994). OS/2 in '94. *OS2 Professional.* 11:7-9.

Bott, E. (March, 1994). Inside Windows 4.0. *PC Computing.* 7:124-139.

Foley, M. Jo. (February 21, 1994). NT slowly winning converts. *PC WEEK.* 11:39.

Goodman, J. M. and Soucha, J. (1993). *DOS 6.0 power tools: Techniques, tricks, and utilities.* New York: Bantam Books.

Kantrowitz. (February, 1994). The metaphor is the message. *Newsweek.* 73:49.

Langa, F. (March, 1994). Win.INI. *Windows Magazine.* 5:11, 14.

Leyenberger, A. (October, 1993). Windows explodes! *Laptop Computers Magazine.* 5:32-37.

Lundgren, T., and Garrett, N. (1994). *Advanced microcomputer applications.* New York: Macmillan.

Salemi, J. (April, 1992). OS/2 2.0-: Does it fulfill the promise? *PC Magazine.* 11:165-192.

Seymour, J. (February, 1994). The service bureau scandal. *PC Magazine.* 13:99-100.

Thompson, T. (January, 1994). Apple provides PC on a Mac. *BYTE.* 19:19.

Wolverton, V. (January, 1994). DOS vs. DOS vs. DOS. *PC World.* 12:171-180.

CHAPTER 13

Computer Network Technology: A Survey of Basic Components, Configurations, and Benefits of Local Area Networks

DENNIS LABONTY

Utah State University, Logan, Utah

As personal computers and software applications become plentiful in classrooms, more and more teachers are faced with management dilemmas. A room full of standalone personal computers, separate printers, multiple application software, and a glut of data disks can quickly become an unruly and exasperating experience. On the other hand, a well-managed local area network (LAN) can be a convenient method of maintaining control.

A well-designed classroom LAN can make hardware and software management easy and efficient. But there are other advantages of using LANs over standalone personal computers (PCs) in the classroom. Understanding these advantages and exploring the inner workings of local area networks have become necessities for business educators with the rapid acceptance of classroom LANs.

This article defines a basic local area network and describes workstations, file servers, and network operating software for a well-designed LAN. In addition, this article describes LAN topologies, cabling, medium control, and application software, and it lists some benefits of classroom LANs.

The best definition of a LAN has been established by the Institute of Electrical and Electronics Engineers (IEEE).

A datacomm system allowing a number of independent devices to communicate directly with each other, within a moderately sized geographic area over a physical communications channel of moderate data rates (Martin, p. 4).

LAN CHARACTERISTICS

Local area networks are characterized by:

- Private ownership
- Moderate data rates
- Short distances
- Low error rates
- Baseband transmission

All of these characteristics make LANs well suited for classroom use. Generally, LANs consist of privately owned hardware and software, and they are maintained privately. For example, a teacher in a business education department may be assigned to be the network administrator and will be solely responsible for management and maintenance of that network.

LAN transmission data rates range from several thousand bits per second (Kbps) to 100 million bits per second (Mbps). One Mbps can be described as a transmission of one million bits of data every second, but speeds from two to 10 Mbps are adequate for most classroom LANs.

The geographic range of a local area network is small—somewhere between 100 yards and 15 miles. The optimum operating distance of LANs is established by industry standards and is based upon network components and end user needs. For example, a thin Ethernet cable network has a maximum trunk segment length of 185 meters and a maximum number of 30 stations connected to that segment. This configuration is ideal for LANs limited to one or two classrooms that contain between 15 and 30 personal computers.

LANs have low error rates because the hardware and software are engineered so that personal computers can be linked together free from electromagnetic interference. In most cases, new connectors, network interface cards, cabling, and software make networks problem free, which was not possible even five years ago.

Virtually all classroom LANs operate as baseband systems, meaning that one message of information at a time can be transmitted over a segment of cable.

LAN COMPONENTS

The primary components of LANS include:

- Workstations
- File servers
- Network interface cards
- Backup systems
- Network operating software

Workstation nodes. On a local area network, a node can be a personal computer, printer, scanner, or other device that is attached to LAN cabling. Nodes are sometimes referred to as workstations. In classroom networks, workstations are generally personal computers.

Personal computers are manufactured with numerous capabilities and endless variations. Although most personal computers manufactured today can be networked together, a prudent network administrator should check with a personal computer manufacturer to determine the networking potential for that model. Some very old models of PCs cannot be networked, and sometimes it is difficult to network PCs that have two different types of operating systems.

DOS compatible personal computers must have a network interface card (NIC) installed in order to connect them to network cabling. When connecting Macintosh computers to Ethernet or token-ring networks, NICs must be installed, too.

Network interface cards. NICs provide several important roles, but one reason for the NIC is that it contains each workstation's address. Information that is communicated on the network is cut up and placed into packets. The size of these packets can vary from 500 to 2,000 bytes. Packets are placed into digital frames that travel along the network cabling. Among other things, including the information packet, frames contain a destination address that either matches or does not match the address of the workstation's NIC. This process is how messages reach the correct workstation for processing.

Interface cards vary in price and capabilities. Ethernet interface cards cost between $70 and $120, and IBM token-ring NICs cost between $420 and $450.

Macintosh computers that are not Ethernet or token-ring networked can be daisy chained together without a NIC. The engineers of Macintosh computers developed a phonenet connector, which is a device that connects telephone wires through the computer's serial output port. A phonenet has two ordinary RJ11 telephone jacks—one for sending out signals and one for receiving signals. In this way, several Macintosh personal computers can be daisy chained together by connecting telephone wires to the phonenet connectors.

Each personal computer on a LAN should have one 3.5-inch high-capacity disk drive bay or each PC should be equipped with both 3.5-inch and 5.25-inch high-capacity disk drive bays. Different disk drive bays give end users the ability to store their information on their own disks.

Personal computer work stations in a well-designed network do not need large amounts of hard disk storage capacity. The file server computer on the network is the device that is responsible for storing most of the application and data software or files. Generally, workstations do not need more than 60 or 120 MB of storage capacity. However, files are exponentially getting larger and hard disk storage is becoming less expensive; consequently, more storage capacity must be considered for future network applications.

The random access memory (RAM) capacity of each workstation should be a minimum of 4MB. A MB is representative of one million bytes. Some application software requires 4MB or 8MB to operate correctly. For example, if the end user wants to run a MicroSoft Windows version of a word processor and manipulate graphics, RAM should be 8MB or more.

Portable and notebook computers are capable of being networked and becoming workstations. As portable and notebook computers are penetrating educational settings, their networking capacity is becoming a more urgent concern. One solution is a wireless network. Laptop and notebook computers can be equipped with radio transmission apparatus much like cellular telephones that "talk" to LANs through router devices.

Printers are an important part of any LAN system, and although many devices can be shared on networks, in classroom settings sharing printers is the biggest concern. It is more efficient and cost effective to share only a few printers than it is to have a classroom with many printers. Paper, toner, and other printer supplies can be strategically located for convenience and access.

On some networks, all printing is controlled by a single personal computer called a print server. These servers are good for managing printing jobs from the workstations. A print server receives the printing assignments from several workstations and apportions and arranges the printing jobs. A print server can perform as a workstation, too.

The number of printers on a LAN needs to be assessed and adjusted to the volume of printing jobs from end users. Generally, two laser printers can fulfill all the printing requirements for about 25-30 workstations.

Dot-matrix printers are adequate for many printing tasks. The cost of maintaining dot-matrix printers is a lot less than the cost of toner and paper for laser printers. When one considers the ultimate disposition of student printouts, lower quality printouts may be adequate for some assignments. However, dot matrix printers are slow and unsatisfactory if the documents' image, quality, and appearance matter.

A well-designed classroom LAN should include high-quality printers for graphics and desktop publishing. High-quality printers include laser, bubblejet, and LED (light-emitted diodes) technology. These printer systems are faster than dot-matrix; therefore, fewer printers are necessary for a network.

File servers. The file server on a server-based network is a personal computer that stores the network operating system software, application software accessible to all end users, and data files created by users. If only one personal computer is used as a file server and it is responsible for all file sharing functions, it is called a "server-based" or "dedicated" system. On the other hand, if each workstation acts as a network file server, the network is called a "peer-to-peer" system. The hardware and operating software requirements for a server-based or peer-to-peer system are different.

File servers are the work horses of networks. They are responsible for distributing files to end users, controlling workstations, maintaining file security, manipulating graphics, and overseeing other network functions. Therefore, they must be high-performance personal computers.

The "top of the line" DOS platform, high-end personal computers contain 66Mhz i486™ DX2 and 60-Mhz Intel Pentium™ processing chips. Mhz means megahertz or millions of electrical cycles per second. The higher the megahertz, the faster the personal computer. DX and DX2 personal computers include a math co-processor; SX personal computers do not. Pentium is the name that Intel selected to call its 586 processor. While 486 chips will process 32 bits at a time, Intel Pentium chips will process 64 bits at a time. Some personal computer manufacturers installed Intel 486 processors with a Pentium Overdrive™ upgrade. This permits a Pentium chip to be added later to a 486 chip for 64-bit processing power.

Personal computers that use 486 or Pentium processors are designed to handle high-end graphic applications. They can be excellent file servers because they are fast and powerful.

Intel's Peripheral Component Interconnect (PCI) is new technology to the personal computer market. PCI is a local-bus graphic chip and works with the Pentium processor chip. When placed together Pentium/PCI is the Porsche of personal computers.

File servers need high-capacity random access memory (RAM) to run graphical software applications. A file server should be equipped with a minimum of 8MB of RAM and upwards to 16MB if using high-end graphical applications.

A file server that supports high-end graphics users should have local-bus architecture and contain as many expansion slots as possible. Local-bus architecture improves the speed that images display on monitors, and expansion slots are necessary to increase network services. Additionally, a file server should be equipped with 3.5-inch and 5.25-inch disk drive bays.

Most LANs have at least one dedicated file server. File servers need large data storage capacity—the larger the better! High-capacity 340MB or 450MB hard drives are not uncommon in classroom LANs of 30 workstations. Newer PC servers are providing hard-disk capacity of 1.2 gigabytes. (A gigabyte is one billion bytes of information.) File servers with 1-3 GB of hard disk space are common in schools in which several classrooms of computers are networked together.

Another storage alternative is to use CD-ROM towers containing 2-14 CDs to store application software. LAN administrators must be cognizant of newer technologies—like CD-ROM among others—that expand storage limits. See Chapter 15 for specific information concerning CD-ROM drive selection recommendations.

Backup systems. Network administrators must design backup procedures into networks. Backing up the file server and the workstation hard drives is an important function.

Hard drive backup systems and magnetic tape backup systems are two affordable alternatives. These systems can quickly save all files on a file server. Once saved, the files can be safely stored or archived at a secure location.

In a well-designed LAN, the file server needs to be safeguarded with an uninterruptible power supply (UPS) device and an antivirus software program. UPSs are manufactured with many protection capabilities. If the network begins to go down because of electrical problems (i.e. sag, spike, or blackout) the UPS can provide enough power to warn end users and back up the file server(s). Only UPSs costing $80 or more are sophisticated enough to provide any protection. Once a power surge occurs, the UPS may indicate that it can no longer provide protection against electrical problems.

Antivirus software provides additional network protection by detecting and removing virus programs that emerge on the network from contaminated disks. Antivirus software should be updated every year if possible so that it protects against the newest viruses that have been created.

Network operating software. The network operating software is the program that enables workstations to share files and peripherals on a network. Many companies manufacture network operating software; each software has individual and proprietary characteristics necessary to control a plethora of network configurations. When selecting a network operating system, a classroom network administrator should consider the following: peer-to-peer vs. server-based LANs, LAN topologies, and brands of personal computers.

It is beyond the scope of this article to compare or list all network operating software; instead only a few examples of network operating software will be listed. Some versatile network operating software includes: Novell Netware, MicroSoft LAN Manager, Artisoft LANtastic, Banyan Vines, MicroSoft Windows NT "new technologies," and MicroSoft Windows NT Advanced Server. Macintosh computers use Appleshare/Appletalk network operating software.

Some network operating software manufacturers recommend that only certain kinds of PCs operate their software. For example, Novell Netware certifies computers that can run its software. A network administrator who wants to run Novell Netware should first check this certified computer list.

LAN TOPOLOGIES, CABLING, AND CONTROL

Topology. Network topology refers to the physical configuration of devices and the cable that connects them. Three standard topologies for classrooms are the bus, ring, and star, which are listed below.

Bus. In a bus topology, each station is attached to one communication cable to transport messages. Each workstation attached to the cable receives messages and determines if the message address is for that workstation. If the workstation recognizes the address, then it processes the message; otherwise it ignores the message. Bus networks are not joined at the endpoints. Instead, terminators are attached to endpoints. It is here that terminators absorb exhausted or useless messages.

An advantage of a bus topology is that workstations can be easily connected or disconnected to the main bus cable without disturbing other workstations. Generally, a bus uses carrier sense multiple access with collision detection (CSMA/CD). This method controls messages and electrical traffic on the transmission medium.

Ethernet is the most widely applied version of bus topology and CSMA/CD. Ethernet is a commercial product originally developed by Xerox Corporation in the early 1970s. Today, Ethernet specifications are cooperatively shared by Digital Equipment Company, Intel Corporation, and Xerox Corporation.

Ring. A ring topology is created with cable that forms a loop. Workstations are attached, and messages travel as electronic signals around the loop. Each workstation looks at the message address to determine if it is to be processed or ignored. In order to prevent the signal from weakening or becoming attenuated, each station acts as a repeater and retransmits the signal at its original strength. IBM supports a token-ring topology.

Token-ring topologies maintain high bit-rate transmission over long distances. However, it can be difficult to connect or disconnect workstations to a token-ring. Therefore, IBM introduced a multiple access unit (MAU). Workstations can be connected to (or disconnected from) a token-ring topology by being plugged into (or unplugged from) a MAU.

Star. In a star topology, all workstations are linked directly to a central controller. Central controllers are called hubs or concentrators. All messages that are communicated between workstations must pass through the hub. These topologies work well with twisted pair wiring or coaxial cables.

Star topologies provide slower but highly reliable bit-rate transmissions; however, they are vulnerable if the hub malfunctions. ARCnet, developed by Datapoint, implements the star topology.

Transmission medium. Transmission medium refers to the type of cabling, connectors, and network interface cards necessary to assemble a LAN. Only the basic types of cabling and connectors will be discussed as network interface cards can be adapted to the type of cable selected for a network.

Coaxial cable consists of a central conducting core, usually copper wire, encased or wrapped in an insulation material. The insulation material consists of one or more layers of nonconducting material to protect the central core from electromagnetic interference. The insulation layer normally contains a layer of material that gives strength to the cable in case it is stretched, twisted, or bent. Coaxial cable provides good protection against electromagnetic interference. Also, it supports data rates up to 100 Mbps.

Twisted pair wiring consists of two insulated copper wires twisted together in a spiral pattern. Each wire in the pair acts as a single communication channel—one sends and one receives. The wires are twisted together to reduce electromagnetic interferences and the closer the twists, the more protected the wire. Several pairs can be bundled together for expandability, and variations of shielded and unshielded protection make this medium suitable for almost any environment. Data rates between 2Mbps and 16Mbps are common on twisted pair networks, but 100Mbps are possible.

Other mediums like fiber optic cable and wireless radio wave and infrared networks are evolving and provide educational potential. Fiber optic cable is more expensive than twisted pair or coaxial cable. Special technicians are needed to install fiber optic cable. Before wireless networks are accepted, health concerns related to them will need to be resolved. Classroom network administrators should keep an eye on these developing technologies for future considerations.

Nodes or workstations are attached to the cable or wiring through special connecting devices. When coaxial cable is used, the connecting devices can be a BNC T connector; or, when twisted pair wiring is used, the connecting devices can be an RJ-11 or RJ-45 phone jack.

Medium access control. Because baseband LANs use only one communication channel, there must be a medium access control technique. In fact, there are three common access control methods: random, distributed, and central control. Each access technique has been successfully developed for different configurations and applications. Together, the network interface card and network operating software are responsible for controlling the transmission medium.

Random access control uses a method that permits all workstations to transmit signals over the transmission channel. If two workstations send messages at the same time, then a collision occurs. Managing collisions is an important component of this procedure. An example of a random access control method is collision sense multiple access with collision detection (CSMA/CD). Bus topologies are good configurations for this technique.

Distributed access control uses a procedure that permits transmission rights to only one workstation at a time. The right to transmit is passed from workstation to workstation through a token. Inasmuch as the token must loop around to each station, this technique works best on a ring configuration, but it is also acceptable on a bus topology.

Central control uses one station or hub to control the entire network. Workstations that are ready to transmit a message must receive permission from the hub. This technique is applicable on star topologies.

LAN APPLICATION SOFTWARE

Software manufacturers will often produce two versions of an application software: a LAN version and a standalone version. Application software for a LAN is designed to allow files to be shared by many end users and is tailored for network intricacies; whereas, standalone versions may not perform optimumly on a network.

Generally, a network administrator can purchase one copy of an application software and a site license. A site license gives the network administrator permission to use as many copies of the application software as there are workstations on the LAN or for a designated number of workstations. Additionally, packages of several copies of an application software can be purchased for a LAN, which is less expensive than purchasing individual programs. Even though many copies of the application software are purchased in packages, only one copy of the program needs to be loaded onto the file server.

Schools can save money by purchasing site licenses or copies of software for fewer computers than the total number on a network. For example, in a community college or university computer lab, a graphics software site license for 10 computers may be purchased rather than a license for every computer on the network. When the eleventh user tries to acces the software, that user is blocked from access to it. For frequently-used software such as word processing software, all workstations should be able to access the software at one time.

LAN BENEFITS

Local area networks connect computers so users can share information, programs, and other costly resources. LANs save money by not requiring as many resources, such as printers. The primary benefits of local area networks include:

- electronic mail
- securing files
- time management
- student information.

Classroom LANs have many advantages. They allow teachers and students to communicate with one another by means of electronic mail. LANs are tools by which teachers can secure and oversee application programs and data disks. LANs enable network administrators and teachers to manage their time and be more efficient in the classroom. LANs can be connected conveniently with other LANs to share information and services over a wide area.

Electronic mail. Electronic mail is becoming a service that LAN users cannot live without. Electronic messages can be efficiently sent and received on a local area network. Conveniently, business teachers can communicate with individual students or transmit one class announcement to everyone.

E-mail software running on a LAN permits users not only to send messages, but also to attach files to messages for transmission. This ability represents another way that files can be shared on a network.

Securing files. Business educators who use LANs can secure and oversee application programs and data disks. This benefit relates to professional ethics.

Due to site licensing laws, software must be protected against illegal use and improper copying. Network administrators can protect software more easily on a LAN than on standalone personal computers. In a room full of standalone personal computers, software must be distributed to students on disks and is vulnerable to being copied, stolen, or damaged. On the other hand, software can be more secure on a network because it can not be handled or touched. The software can be accessed by authorized students and teachers only from the file server, where it is safely stored. For example, in an accounting class, only students with authorized usernames and passwords can access the accounting software, but not other software.

Time management. A well-designed LAN can provide more time for business educators. Teachers struggle to manage their time. Educational responsibilities require many hours of work, and steps that "free up" any amounts of time are welcomed.

When asked about the advantages of using a LAN, K. C. Jones, a network administrator and business educator for Skyview High School in Smithfield, Utah, observed, "You only have to load or upgrade software once!" Peggy Ross, business educator at Bozeman High School, Bozeman, Montana, commented, "Loading, clearing, and replacing programs is easier on a network!"

If a software upgrade requires 20 minutes of installation time, five hours would be required for a teacher to upgrade 15 standalone personal computers —the same software could be installed on the file server in 20 minutes.

Additional time can be saved as fewer printers need to be serviced and maintained. Also, teachers are not burdened with disks to distribute and collect during each class meeting.

Another time-saving benefit of a LAN is that everyone uses the same software. Students using standalone personal computers can individually customize their application software, thereby making teacher demonstrations more difficult because everyone in the classroom could be working on a differently configured screen. On a LAN, all software is configured the same, which converts into more time for classroom teaching.

Student information. LANs can be tools to collect, analyze, and report student information. Special network software has been developed by software and personal computer manufacturers that do the following: record student grades onto a database; compute student attendance records throughout the school year; and compile and send student progress reports. These services are fast, accurate, and benefit everyone.

Another dimension of special education LAN software is that it can control workstations in the classroom. For example, a teacher can access a student's monitor from the teacher's monitor to watch how that student performs an activity; or a teacher can demonstrate a lesson by broadcasting what is on his/her monitor onto students' monitors; or a teacher can lock workstation keyboards so as not to be interrupted during a demonstration with students pecking away at a game or another activity.

IBM sells an education network package called IBM Education LAN and Tools 386 (EdLAN 386). It contains seven software programs including IBM Classroom LAN Administration System Version 1.40 (ICLAS) for security, print queue management, tape backup, and simplified network installation; LAN School for workstation display control; and Excelsior Grade2 for grade books. These utility programs are for networks of 50 or 100 users and 50 machines.

LAN connectivity. A recent advantage of local area networks is their connectivity. Connecting LANs together, connecting to the Internet, and accessing commercial databases should be incorporated into a well-designed LAN.

In other words, a LAN not only should expand by adding additional workstations, but also should be conceived with the ability to connect to other LANs. It is becoming increasingly easier to connect two or more LANs together. Devices called repeaters, bridges, and routers (brouters) allow messages to be sent from one LAN to another.

Some schools are connecting several LANs within the same building, whereas other schools are connecting LANs between schools. This expansion creates a wide area network (WAN). WANs save money for school districts by developing an information sharing infrastructure.

Also, well-designed LANs should be prepared with the capability to gateway into public data networks like the Internet. The Internet is the largest international network of computers. There are many information services available on the Internet, and it is a good classroom tool for business educators and business education students. A gateway is a dedicated personal computer that routes messages throughout complex networks.

LANs can be expanded to include commercial databases and services like CompuServe, Prodigy, or American Online. These databases can be accessed from a LAN workstation through a modem server.

SUMMARY

Unfortunately some classroom networks have been put together without planning or foresight. At other times, network components were dumped upon business teachers with the idea that networks can be easily assembled. These ill-fated events negatively affect network performance.

But many business educators are discovering that well-designed local area networks can facilitate instruction through better managed equipment and software. LANs are important, and they are becoming more important as personal computers and software applications saturate classrooms. LANs can help business educators to improve their instruction, to oversee their equipment and software, and to teach students about personal computers for careers in business. Also, LANs can save much time, effort, and frustration when managing a room of personal computers.

REFERENCES

Abernathy, J. (January, 1994). 7 Pentiums for less than $3500. *PC World, 12*(1), 70-73.

Andre, E. (November, 1993). Network printing: Past, present, and future. *Network Computing, 4*(12), 99-116.

Cohen, A. M. (1991). *A guide to networking.* Boston: Boyd & Fraser Publishing Company, a division of South-Western Publishing Company.

Gerber, B. (July, 1992). Selecting servers. *Network Computing, 3*(7), 85-101.

Magidson, S. (May, 1992). Portable computing: Managing the nework connection. *Network Computing, 3*(5), 71-79.

Martin, J. (1989). *Local area networks.* Englewood Cliffs, NJ: Prentice Hall Publishing Company.

Ramos, E. & Schroeder, A. (1994). *Concepts of data communications.* New York: Macmillan Publishing Company.

Smith, B. & Udell, J. (December, 1993). Linking LANs. *BYTE, 18*(13), 66-90.

CHAPTER 14

Implementing and Troubleshooting a Classroom LAN

MARCIA JAMES
University of Wisconsin-Whitewater, Whitewater, Wisconsin

In this era of tight school budgets, local area networks (LANs) afford schools a means for maximizing classroom computer resources.

LANs allow students to share information (files), software programs, and peripherals (i.e., printers). This sharing of resources saves money on hardware and software. Although LANs can save money for a school, they also present challenges to those individuals—often business teachers—who are asked to select LAN technology, and manage, use, and troubleshoot the classroom LANs. According to a 1994 survey of business education state supervisors, in most states the business teacher is responsible for setting up and maintaining classroom LANs.*

This chapter offers teachers some guidelines for selecting LAN hardware and software and managing, using, and troubleshooting a local area network.

GUIDELINES FOR SELECTING LAN HARDWARE AND SOFTWARE

A school can "tap" some or all of the services of a vendor when selecting LAN hardware and software. Procuring a LAN is a three-step process: designing the LAN, requesting bids on hardware and software, and installing the LAN.

Step 1: Designing the LAN. Many vendors offer a fee-based service which includes designing a LAN for present and future networking needs. Once a school contracts with a vendor to have a LAN designed, the vendor meets with school officials (a technology committee) to determine the goals and objectives of the school. The vendor considers those goals along with the proposed budget, and the constraints of the facility. After careful study, the vendor prepares a document which designates the topology (layout) of the network but avoids specifying hardware and software.

The two most common topologies used are the ring (token ring) and bus (Ethernet). A third topology is a star. While the IBM Token Ring runs internally as a ring topology, it appears physically to be a star topology. For classroom LANs, 16 megabytes-per-second Token Ring networks are faster but more expensive than 10 megabytes-per-second Ethernet networks.

The survey of business education supervisors indicated that schools are

---

*Before writing this chapter, the author surveyed business education state supervisors from all states. Twenty-five surveys were returned for a 50 percent response rate.

more concerned with the cost of the network than with the speed of data transmission. Ethernet was cited by 52 percent of the business education state supervisors as the most popular network in their state; token ring was cited by only 18 percent of the respondents. The other respondents indicated that their networks were a combination of token ring and Ethernet networks, were another kind of network, or they did not know their type of network.

Other factors that might affect the configuration of the network are information services such as CompuServe, an e-mail system, and the Internet. These services enable users to communicate outside of the constraints of LANs; therefore, they require additional hardware and software considerations.

The choice of vendor is critical in the first step of the three-step process. School officials should contact other school districts and customers of potential vendors for recommendations. Finding out the track record of a vendor early in the design stage can avoid pitfalls in the subsequent steps of the selection process.

Step 2: Requesting bids on hardware and software. Using the design constructed by a vendor, requests for bids on hardware and software should be solicited.

The following questions should be answered in each vendor's bid proposal:

1. What is the brand of network hardware (i.e., IBM Token Ring, 10BaseT Ethernet, 3Com, etc.)?

2. What is the brand of network operating system software (i.e., Novell Netware, OS/2 Lan Server, or AppleTalk)?

3. What is the brand of workstations and the configuration of them (RAM memory, hard disk space, type & speed of microprocessor)?

4. What type of cable does the network require (i.e., shielded or unshielded twisted pair, coaxial, or fiber optic)?

5. What is the speed of data transmission (i.e., 10 megabytes per second or 16 megabytes per second)?

6. What is the access time of users on the network?

7. What is the brand/type of file server computer (Macintosh, IBM compatible, or UNIX)?

8. What is the configuration of the file server(s):
   a. type of microprocessor—486 or Pentium,
   b. the amount of random access memory (12-16 megabytes), and
   c. the size of the hard disk (1-3 gigabytes)?

9. How many servers are needed (networks have a ratio of a number of workstations per server such as 40:1)?

10. How many workstations can be supported on one network?

11. How many networks are needed and how many bridges or routers are needed to connect the LANs together?

12. How many network interface cards are needed? Or are they pre-installed in the computer workstations, as they are in some models of Macintosh computers?

13. How much and what type of cabling will be used?

14. How many hubs are needed for Ethernet networks or MAUs, CAUs or LAMs for IBM Token Ring networks?

15. What type of backup system (tape backup) is needed?

16. What type of uninterruptible power supply (UPS) is included in the bid?

17. How many school personnel will be trained to administer the LAN? How many days of training will be provided?

Types of networks. Before requesting bids from vendors, a school's technology committee should become familiar with local area network components. The following sections provide an overview of essential LAN hardware and software components.

The two major types of networks are peer-to-peer and server based networks. A peer-to-peer network does not require that a computer be dedicated to performing network tasks. All the computers are used as workstations. The most popular peer-to-peer network at this time is Lantastic. Peer-to-peer networks are less expensive than server-based networks, but are not as popular as server-based networks in businesses or schools.

A network with a dedicated file server is more expensive but more efficient than a peer-to-peer network. All network operating system software and network versions of application software are stored on the file server computer. In schools, security of data on the network is better with a server-based network than a peer-to-peer network; in fact, the file server computer is often kept in a locked office rather than in the classroom.

File servers. Depending upon the number of workstations a network can support, at least one server should be purchased. If a network carries a heavy printing load, one server can be designated for printing documents while another can manage the network and provide applications and files.

The server(s) can be located in the same room as the network or in another room or building. The location is dependent upon the type of network and the proximity to the network administrator. Server-based networks should have the server in a private office so that the administrator can install software or run diagnostics while classes are using the network.

If only one server is purchased, the unit is dedicated to providing applications and files, managing the printer requests, and enabling the network administrator to perform network maintenance tasks.

Although it is not necessary to buy a color monitor for the server, the computer processing unit should possess a fast microprocessor and plenty of random access memory so that the unit can operate efficiently. Also, a large disk drive is necessary for storing programs and files. Finally, an internal or external backup unit should be purchased to make a second copy of important applications and files.

Cabling. Three forms of cabling can be used for networks: twisted pair wire, coaxial cable, and fiber optic cable. The least expensive and easiest to work with is twisted pair wire. It comes in two types: unshielded twisted pair (UTP) and shielded twisted pair (STP). Problems with noise on the network from fluorescent lights and copiers are more prevalent with unshielded twisted pair. Twisted pair wire is the easiest and most flexible to install. Fiber optic cable requires a trained technician for installation and is the most expensive. Both IBM Token Ring networks and 10BaseT Ethernet networks use twisted pair cable.

Computer workstations. Workstations are the computers used by students on the network. Workstations, also called nodes, should have their own hard disk drive for several reasons. For example, graphic programs need a location for temporary files. If a workstation has its own hard disk, the temporary files can be placed locally rather than transmitted to the server. Also, if the network "goes down," the students can work on application programs that are available on individual workstations.

Workstations should have a color monitor, a fast microprocessor chip (not necessarily as fast as the chip in the file server), a mouse or trackball, and an ergonomically correct environment to promote efficient computing.

Network interface cards. A network interface card (adapter cards) is placed in the central processing unit (CPU) of each work station and each file server. These cards allow the network cabling to connect to each computer workstation and file server. Network interface cards are designed for a specific type of network (network protocol). For example, one type of interface card is designed for 10BaseT Ethernet networks that use twisted pair wire; a second type card is for Ethernet networks that use coaxial cable; a third type for IBM Token Ring networks, and a fourth type for AppleShare (Macintosh) networks.

Network connectivity hardware. In order to connect workstations and peripherals together on a network other equipment is needed. Even the smallest IBM Token Ring network requires an additional purchase—a multiple access unit (MAU). This type of network is called a "token ring" because the cable is in a ring inside the MAU, and data is transmitted around the ring via a token (an electronic collection plate). To transmit or receive data, a computer or printer must hold the token.

All the workstations on a network are plugged into RJ-45 ports on a MAU. When more workstations are added on relatively small token ring networks, one or more additional MAUs must be purchased. When two or more MAUs are used, a ring-out port on one MAU is connected to the next MAUs ring-in port; the last ring-out port is connected back to the first MAUs ring-in port, thereby creating the "ring." A MAU costs between $350 and $450.

On large IBM Token Ring networks, MAUs are being replaced by CAUs (8230 Controlled Access Units). CAUs are considered intelligent wiring concentrators and act very much like hubs on Ethernet networks. The 8230 CAU is a base unit, typically kept in a wiring closet, and contains wiring modules. The 8230 CAU can contain up to four 8230 CAU LAMs (lobe attachment modules). With the use of these concentrators, up to 260 workstations can be on a ring. In the future, it may be possible to attach even more workstations.

With 10BaseT Ethernet networks, a hub is needed for small networks with 16 or fewer workstations. A hub provides the ports needed to attach workstations to the network—one port for each workstation. A hub acts as an Ethernet repeater, connects workstations to the network, and enforces collision detection. A fiberoptic Ethernet LAN (10BASE-FL) is often used for larger networks with the workstations connected to a central concentrator or repeater. A ThinNet Ethernet LAN (10Base2) uses a multiport repeater to connect workstations.

Other expenditures. An ergonomically correct environment includes: task lighting, computer desks, adjustable chairs, static diffusing carpet, noise shields for impact printers, and a heating system with a humidifier. In many geographical locations, air conditioning may be a requirement.

Other purchases the school may want to consider include:

- an uninterrupted power supply (UPS) to prevent power interruptions (brownouts and blackouts) from affecting computing
- a portable telephone for troubleshooting workstations with off-site service personnel
- an internal or external modem
- a repeater to extend the length of an Ethernet LAN or the distance between MAUs.
- a local bridge/router to join LANs in a single building or campus
- a remote bridge to connect networks in different cities
- router to connect two identical LANs together
- locked storage cupboards for backup copies of software
- an off-site, climate-controlled environment for original copies of software
- bookcases for documentation.

A plastic sleeve can be positioned on the side of a monitor to hold a reference diskette that is specific to that workstation. Also, computers and printers should be secured to the work surfaces by cables with key or combination locks to prevent theft.

Printers. Shared printers are a popular benefit of networking. Students can select one of several printers on a network to print documents. Some printers and other peripherals are not networkable. Those that are can be connected to the server that has the responsibility for controlling documents being sent to networked printers. The printers must possess sufficient memory for spooling (holding documents in memory while waiting their turn for printing). Hewlett Packard as well as a few other companies have special "network printers" on the market because using regular laser printers on networks has caused so many problems.

Cabling. Workstations, peripherals, and servers can be connected using traditional cabling methods (twisted pair wires, coaxial cables, fiber optics) or using wireless methods (radio waves or laser beams). Some brands and/or types of networks require a specific type of cabling. Twisted pair has several advantages over the other two types of cable. Twisted pair is easier to install and is usually less expensive than coaxial cable and fiber optic. Anyone can be trained to attach connectors to twisted pair wire, but a skilled technician is needed to install (pull) fiber optic cable. Coaxial cable is bulkier and less flexible than twisted pair wire. Fiber optic cable is the most expensive, but also transmits data the fastest and can transmit data, voice, and video simultaneously.

Disk operating system software. Software selection includes disk operating systems (DOS), network operating systems, and application software. The disk operating system (i.e., MS-DOS, Macintosh's System, or UNIX) selected will depend on the brand of computer workstations that will be used. The business education supervisors who were surveyed indicated that most states use MS-DOS as their primary operating system environment.

Hardware prices. According to Schramm and Moses (1994), the file server should have at least a 486 processor, which can cost between $2,000 and $3,000. Computers with faster processors such as a Pentium processor cost more but are recommended highly. Many of these chips can process data at 60-100 megahertz(mhz). Network interface (adapter) cards range in price between $150 and $300, and network cables cost from $10-$300, depending on the length needed. All servers and workstations require network interface cards and cables. Workstation computers were quoted by Schramm and Moses to cost between $1,000 and $2,000. Teachers should be aware that hardware costs seem to be going down each year except for brand-new technologies.

Network operating system software. The network operating system (i.e., Novell Netware, IBM's OS/2 Lan Server, and AppleTalk) is less dependent upon the network hardware selected because of technological advancements. Therefore, the features of the network operating system software should be given primary consideration in the selection process. Network operating system software acts as the traffic cop on the network allowing messages and documents to be sent from one computer to another without having data collisions. This software also allows the network administrator to set up directories for users and run diagnostics to locate network problems. Without network operating system software, none of the hardware components would be able to "talk" to each other.

Application software. The choice of hardware, operating system, and network operating system software should be driven by the goals and objectives of the school. However, the application software (word processing, spreadsheet, and database) should be selected based upon the needs of prospective employers. Since students move from city to city and state to state, national software trends can be used as a guide when selecting software. Before application software is purchased, some key questions need to be asked:

• What are the most popular application programs?

• Which disk operating system does the application software require?

• Is a network version of the application software available?

• How much hard disk space and how much RAM memory is needed by the application software?

• Is a specific release of operating system software required to run the application software?

• Does the application software require Microsoft Windows? If so, which release?

Graphical user environments. Operating systems provide the interface between the hardware, the software, and the user. Recent versions are becoming much more powerful and user friendly. Many computer operators do not interface with an MS-DOS operating system, even though it is running in the background, instead they interface with a graphical user environment such as Microsoft Windows. Although the graphical user interface (GUI) was pioneered by Xerox, Microsoft made it an industry standard with its Windows software.

Microsoft Windows makes the process of accessing applications invisible to students. For instance, students may open a desktop publishing program and be unaware that it resides on their own hard disk. Or they may select a word processing program and be unaware that it resides on the file server.

Using Microsoft Windows on a network raises several questions: Should the network version of Windows, Windows NT, be installed on the file server? Should Windows be stored on the hard disk of each individual work station? The pros and cons of each method should be investigated. Discussions with schools that use Windows can be useful.

Step 3: Installing the LAN. Once the vendors of hardware and software are selected, a school should select the party who will install the network. An on-site employee should assist in the installation of the LAN. The employee can log the steps the installer takes to set up hardware, install software, test computers to operate independently, test computers as servers or workstations on the network, set up peripherals, and test the peripherals as devices on the network. This information is valuable for future reference when problems occur or when new software needs to be installed at a later time. The school employee who assists with the installation can also act as liaison between the installer and the school district.

A school employee should be aware of the importance of documenting the address of each network interface card and the location of the computer with that card. This can be invaluable when switching computers, adding computers, or troubleshooting problems. Some network operating systems automatically recognize the address of each workstation (node).

Wiring may be done by an electrician or the installer. The wiring needs to be housed in a wiring closet that can be securely locked. Wiring closets are used to house hubs for Ethernet networks and CAUs and LAMs for IBM Token Ring networks. All workstations on a network are connected by cable to these hubs or CAUs. A coding system for identifying which cable links to which computer should be developed and used.

The vendor who installs the network should be selected for its reputation and service contracts. For example, one vendor offers the following options: no contract, first come first serve, and round the clock service—seven days a week. For a higher price, the company will guarantee an operational network within 24 hours.

From the survey of business education state supervisors, some unique approaches to service problems were revealed. Three states reported that a second server was purchased; and if the first server failed, the second one was attached to the network. Even more states indicated that servers were being equipped with modems so that telephone lines and special software would allow the service person to troubleshoot the network without being on-site.

MANAGING THE NETWORK

The administration of a network is dependent upon the network administrator, the server(s), and the networking operating system.

Network administrator. The individual in charge of network administration should also be the employee who was with the vendor when the network was installed. This network administrator can then understand the positioning of cables, the configuration of the hardware, and the steps to install software on the server and workstations.

A plan for backup of programs, hardware security, off-site storage of original programs, and a log of problems are the initial concerns of the network administrator. Providing virus protection at each workstation and "log on" information at each workstation is also important.

Network operating system. Knowing how to use the features of a network operating system requires training. The network administrator should receive several days of training on the brand of network operating system that is installed. Provisions for training the network administrator can be part of the bidding process described earlier. Ideally, more than one person should be trained so that at least two people are network proficient. If the business teacher is one of the network administrators, release time from teaching duties should be granted by the administration.

According to the 1994 survey of business education state supervisors, 90 percent of the respondents indicated that their states are adopting Novell's Netware as their network operating system.

Whichever network operating system is selected, it should perform functions such as:

- Print management—displays a list of files that have been sent to each printer and the order in which they were sent.

- Software metering—monitors the authorized number of software licenses and prevents more users than the authorized number from accessing the software.

- Password protection—lets the network administrator assign rights to those who should be able to access applications and files, preventing some users from accessing and/or changing certain files.

Large school systems hire computer technicians to select, install, and troubleshoot hardware and software. Their duties and responsibilities vary depending on the school system's needs. However, technicians or the network administrator should show teachers how to use the network.

USING THE NETWORK

Newly licensed business teachers are being prepared at some universities in network administration. Those teachers who graduated "before networks" find themselves back in the classroom.

Universities, technical colleges, and businesses are offering classes and seminars in network administration. Some of these institutions offer certification for those individuals who complete instruction and pass tests in the following areas: adding and deleting user groups, backing up the file server, creating and debugging login scripts, loading application software, maintaining network security, configuring printers, and troubleshooting the network.

Students also need to have some basic network knowledge; they should have instruction on how to "log on" to a computer, how to access programs, how to store files, how to select a printer, how to send a document to a printer, and who to inform if there is a malfunction. Finally, students should be instructed on how to leave the workstation. For example, an instruction sheet can be laminated and adhered to the workstation. This sheet can list how to shut down the computer.

Getting the printer to work correctly. Assuming that the printer functions as a standalone device and is connected properly to the server and the network, there are several reasons why a printer may not function on the network. First, when the network is set up, printer drivers are installed on the server, and the printers are labeled for easy selection by the network users. If the drivers are present and the printer is made available to network users, the printer should work.

Next, the network administrator should ensure that the printer has been configured correctly. For example, some printers require parallel ports whereas others require serial ports. Also, the correct printing cable is necessary for communication between the server and the printer.

Another common barrier to printing on the network is using a printer that automatically emulates different modes. For instance, some printers can automatically toggle between postscript and nonpostscript printing. Since documents back up in the queue and mode changes can compound, sometimes the only option is to restart the network.

Wise printer management may prevent overburdening of the print queue. For instance, students may be given printing time or may be instructed to send documents to a specific printer—to disperse the work load.

A network operating system has a print manager feature that lets the network administrator control printer job queues and printer problems—out of paper, paper jams, and no paper tray. Depending upon the sophistication of the network operating system, diagnosing the printer problem may be easier on some networks than on others.

Improving the speed of operations on the network. Three factors affect the speed of printing and of accessing files and other network services:

1. data transmission speed

2. configuration of the server

3. configuration of the workstations and peripherals.

How many megabytes the network can carry per session affects data transmission. Two types of IBM Token Ring networks can be purchased—one runs at 4 megabytes per second (Mbps) and the other at 16 Mbps. High speed data transmission is important for the success of a network. If opening a copy of WordPerfect on students' home computers takes two seconds, then students will expect the time required to open networked versions to be comparable. The only way to keep the network start-up time comparable to the speed of a standalone is to use network adaptors and cable systems that are capable of high-speed performance. An investment in the 16 megabytes per second Token Ring network or a 10 megabytes per second Ethernet network is recommended.

The configuration of the server affects the efficiency of the network. For instance, a fast processor, sufficient random access memory, and a large hard disk are necessary. Similarly, the configurations of the workstations and peripherals need to be considered for maximizing the network.

Students should be instructed to store files on their own floppy disks so that the local hard drive can be used for software and temporary files. If large documents or graphics are being sent to a printer, students should be instructed to print those documents when the LAN is not used heavily.

TROUBLESHOOTING THE NETWORK

If a network management plan is developed, troubleshooting the network will ease the workload of the network administrator. The plan should accomplish two things: prevent network problems when possible, and prepare for those problems that inevitably occur. Because no two networks are exactly alike, no two network management plans can be the same.

In most cases, a network management plan should address the following areas:

- monitoring and controlling hard disk space usage
- monitoring server workload and performance
- adding and maintaining user log-in identifications and workstation information
- checking and resetting network devices on a regular basis
- performing regular maintenance on databases and other software stored on servers
- making regular backups of files stored on the server
- changing the password on a regular basis.

However, a good plan sometimes fails. When that happens, a decision to call for service is made. Before a service call is made, the following steps should be completed:

1. Document the problem. The service person needs background information on the network. Recurring problems should be logged. New problems can usually be attributed to an easily diagnosed and solvable situation. For instance, if a workstation had been functional on the network but is not working now, disconnected cables and loose connections could be the problem.

2. Discuss the problem with other network users and administrators. Sometimes talking to others can aid in solving the problem.

3. When available, use a reference diskette or another diagnostic tool to determine if the problem is with the unit itself—rather than with the network.

4. If the problem is with the network, use the network operating system features that allow diagnosis of a network problem.

5. If available, use a network diagnostic package that can be used to monitor and correct network malfunctions. These monitoring systems range in price based on the sophistication of the system. Features of some of these systems include statistics on network traffic, detection of overloaded segments, and detailed descriptions of network problems. In addition to detecting network operation problems, some systems detect faulty cables and software viruses. Hand-held cable testers can be useful also.

If the above steps do not solve the problem, the network administration should call for service. Many problems can be solved over the telephone if a network-proficient person is able to follow the verbal instructions of the service people and thus save an expensive on-site service call.

TECHNOLOGICAL TRENDS

When asked what technological trends are occurring in their states, the majority of the business education state supervisors responded: instructional technology, distance education, and Internet connectivity.

Instructional technology, which includes multimedia software, laser disc players, and CD-ROM technology, is making teaching and learning visually exciting. Although Missouri reported a proliferation of multimedia packages, the challenge, as with network administration, is for the business educator to find the time and the resources to implement these new instructional tools.

State supervisors in Idaho and Ohio reported that telecommunications is having an impact on teaching and learning. Areas in these states which were previously inaccessible to educational programs are now able to participate in distance learning.

The Internet brings people together electronically and gives them easy access to each other and to the information and services they want and need. Tresko (1993) describes the Internet as a loosely bound organization of about 10,000 computer networks in 50 countries. As educators prepare students for and about business, students need to know how to use the Internet as they may find themselves using it to compete in a global economy as well as to order a toaster.

Nebraska's business education state supervisor reported that a legislative bill was passed to support the use of tax dollars to connect Educational Service Units to the Internet. This bill will generate over one and one-half million dollars.

Local area networks may become overshadowed by Wide Area Networks (WANs), at least until teachers have a better perspective of the true educational value and need to use e-mail and the Internet. Using off-site services such as CompuServe, e-mail, and the Internet calls for additional hardware and software planning. When these services are added to a network, the school and the network administrator must deal with hardware and software selection issues as well as managing, using, and troubleshooting these additional services.

Educators will need to keep up to date on new networking technologies as networks become an essential tool in educational institutions.

REFERENCES

Entre Computer, personal interview. January, 1994.

Lawrence, B. (1992). *Using Novell netware,* Carmel, Indiana: Que Corporation.

Schramm, R., and Moses, D. R. (1994). *Developing and teaching computer network administration in the business education curriculum.* Manuscript accepted for publication.

Tresko, J. (August 1993). Tripping down the information superhighway. *Industry Week.* p. 32-40.

CHAPTER 15

CD-ROM Devices in the Classroom

KATHI TULLY
Olathe District Schools, Olathe, Kansas

The CD-ROM is one of the most popular technologies for computers in and out of the classroom. Literally thousands of titles are available, although many are not designed for instructional use.

A CD-ROM device is one type of compact disc; however, there are many variations of compact discs including the following:

- CD-ROM – compact disc read-only memory
- Audio CD – audio (music) compact disc
- Photo CD – compact disc containing scanned standard 35mm photographs
- CD-R – rewritable compact optical disc
- CD-I – interactive viewing of audio and video or full motion video
- WORM – write-once, read many archival storage.

Of those various types of compact disc technologies, the CD-ROM is used most frequently. Electronic encyclopedias were the first products used in schools and homes. Products now include application software, video clips, clip art, massive databases and many others. The data stored on a CD-ROM can be loaded into memory, displayed on the screen, or printed, just like data from any other disk drive.

Leslie Eiser (April 1993) provides an explanation of how a CD-ROM drive operates:

> A CD-ROM drive, like the audio CD player on which it's based, consists of a spindle like that of a record player, a laser light source, a lens, and firmware (software instructions built into the drive itself). Light is bounced off the underside of a spinning CD and reflected into the lens, after which the firmware translates the flickering light into a digital signal. This signal can be stored in a buffer in the drive or transferred immediately to the host computer to which the CD-ROM is attached.

Audio CDs can be used on a CD-ROM drive attached to the computer. They can be accessed interactively as part of a multimedia presentation or played in the background while using the computer for word processing or other purposes.

Photo CDs can be used with a standard CD-ROM drive. The drive must have multisession capability if you want the flexibility of adding multiple rolls of photographs at different times. If you have a single session disc, you can only use the photographs from the first printing.

Erasable optical disc drives are now available and are expected to have a major impact on secondary storage. These discs can be used to archive files in a business or save graphic files or video images. Optical discs can store far more data than computer diskettes. A 1.4 megabyte diskette may hold one or two graphic images, but uncompressed digital video requires 22 megabytes of storage per second. Removable optical discs can store as much as a large hard drive and are as easy to change as a diskette.

The price of an erasable optical disc drive is a disadvantage. However, the convenience and the storage capacity far outweigh this disadvantage, and as with all technology, the price is expected to drop in the future.

CD-Interactive (CD-I) allows the viewing of 72 minutes of VHS+ quality and full-motion video using a television set and a CD-I player. This technology was designed primarily for education, training, and entertainment. Many sources predict that this medium will replace the VHS video tapes used in the movie rental industry. Disc-based magazines are also available in the CD-I format.

CD-ROM discs and CD-ROM disc drives offer an increasingly economical distribution medium for read-only data and programs. Write-once, read many (WORM) drives enable organizations to create their own in-house archival databases. Since the discs cannot be altered, it is possible that accounting records may legally be stored on these discs in the future.

NETWORKING CD-ROM DEVICES

Rather than purchasing a CD-ROM drive for each computer attached to a network, many schools save money and increase access to CD-ROMs by networking their CD-ROM drives. CDs can be networked using any of the following three methods:

- Attaching a CD-ROM to individual workstations
- Attaching a CD-ROM to a dedicated computer
- Attaching a CD-ROM to a new or existing fileserver

A CD-ROM drive attached to an individual workstation on a network has a slow response time. This method is only recommended for low use of the CD.

A CD-ROM drive can be attached to a dedicated computer (dedicated to CD-ROM use) on a network, but the computer cannot be used as a workstation. Rather than attach a CD-ROM to a workstation, it can be connected to a file server on a computer network, the preferred method of attaching a CD-ROM to a network.

At this time, up to 28 CD-ROM drives can be attached to a single file server on a network. Multiple servers can be connected to provide unlimited access to CDs. With this method complications may arise. Each workstation must load specific terminate-and-stay-resident (TSR) instructions to attach to the CD. This decreases the amount of memory available at each individual workstation. These TSR instructions may need to be unloaded to use other network applications, making the user go through more steps to switch from CD-ROM applications to word processing, for example.

Several hardware concerns must be addressed when using CD-ROM drives on a network. Additional expansion slots are necessary when attaching CD-ROM drives to a file server. Additional hard disk storage and RAM memory is also necessary. A high speed file server is imperative when networking CD-ROM drives.

One device that may seem to facilitate the use of CD-ROM drives is a six-slot mini-changer CD-ROM drive system. (More than six slots may be available in the future.) This system offers an individual workstation the use of six CD-ROM products without changing discs. On a network, however, this type of drive can prove to be a problem if each network user requests access to a different disc. The drive can become tied up by changing discs in the cartridge.

A better approach for the multiuser is a tower of CD drives with different discs loaded into each. Multiple users can access different CDs without disc-swapping becoming an issue. CD-ROMs on a network require thoughtful planning to ensure appropriate response time and access.

CD-ROM SPECIFICATIONS

Hardware compatibility issues have plagued CD-ROM systems, creating headaches for those purchasing multimedia computers and those adding CD-ROM drives, sound boards, and drivers to older computers. To help alleviate some of those headaches, in 1990 the Multimedia PC (MPC) Marketing Council (Arachtingi, January 1994) established a PC hardware standard for the development of multimedia applications, including the following requirements for a CD-ROM drive:

- Average access times
- Average data transfer rates
- Data buffer sizes
- Mean Time Before Failure (MTBF) rates
- Compatible audio outputs
- Volume control on the front of the drive.

Access time is the time it takes to read information on a disc. An average access or seek time of 1,000ms (milliseconds)or less is required. Double speed drives currently fall under 300ms while hard drives have an access time only in the 9ms to 30ms range. Many packages will not run with access times greater than 360ms. The average data transfer rate must be a minimum of 250-300KB/sec. This is the combination of data and time between the disc and the computer. Standard or single-speed drives with the transfer rate of 150KB/sec are facing obsolescence quickly. Double-speed drives currently are standard (300KB/sec). While triple and quadruple-speed drives (600KB/sec) are available, they can be expensive.

Data buffers are the actual memory locations in the drive or interface card. A minimum of 64K is required for any multimedia program. New drives have up to 256K buffers.

Mean Time Before Failure compares the reliability of products. MTBF statements are listed in specs for VCRs, video cameras, laser players, CD-ROM drives, televisions and computers. CD-ROM drives should have approximately 25,000 hours of MTBF. Newer models are listing 50,000 hours. A drive should have a good warranty if this number is low.

Compatible audio outputs and volume control requirements should be a concern. All products should list requirements to run. Soundcards that are compatible with most CD-ROMs include Soundblaster, Soundblaster Pro, and Thunderboard.

In the immediate future, compatibility of CD-ROM drives and their related peripherals will continue to be a concern.

CD-ROM APPLICATION PROGRAMS

Through the use of CD-ROM applications, students can experience active, nonlinear, and visual instruction. They can explore enormous amounts of data using these methods. CD-ROM applications can provide students with a variety of instructional methods.

For effective usage in business and computer courses, teachers may need to create assignments related to the content of some popular CDs. Compton's Multimedia Encyclopedia, Grolier's Electronic Encyclopedia, and Infotrac were shown to be the most popular CD-programs in North Carolina school library media centers, according to a research project completed in 1993 (Carol Truett, February 1994). These CDs can be used in general business, consumer economics, and other business classes if the instructors create assignments that utilize the CDs.

Software that requires massive disk space is often sold in CD-ROM format rather than on disks. Software stored in CD-ROM format makes previewing, purchasing, and delivery much less burdensome for the consumer. Users can test, purchase, and install software without leaving their office or home. Multiple software packages can be stored on a single CD-ROM disc. If users decide to purchase a product, they can call a toll-free number and receive the code to unlock and install software and documentation on the computer. Installation from a CD is much faster and allows for unattended installation.

Education is a large market for CD products. Advantages include lower shipping rates and less storage space. The shipping charges and storage space requirements are much lower for one CD compared to a standard set of encyclopedias. Other advantages include the allure of an interactive multimedia encyclopedia that plays videos showing major historical events and that allows one to jump from one topic to another with the click of the mouse button. In a video intensive society, student interest in education may improve because information presented in audio or video clips is more appealing.

The largest use of CD products in education is for data bases, indexes to data, and interactive text and graphics. Student research is now much more appealing. While some students have been reluctant to review large amounts of printed material, they may be inclined to browse numerous abstracts and articles on a computer. To search massives databases, students must not only know how to use CD-ROMs but also use problem-solving and critical thinking skills.

CD AND LASER DRIVES

Both external and internal CD drives are available. Internal devices take up less desktop space than external drives. However, external drives are easily transferred from one machine to another provided the same interface is available on both machines. Drives are available with or without caddies; caddyless systems have slide-out trays.

At this time SCSI (Small Computer System Interface) is the interface of choice. This interface standard allows multiple SCSI devices to interact successfully.

Students and teachers should learn proper care and handling of CDs. CDs should be stored in individual caddies or in their plastic case when not in use. While CDs can be held on the edges, users should avoid setting the CD on the desktop as data is written on the bottom of the CD.

Laser discs are built on the same concept as a CD except that they use a larger disc. Drives for a laser disc are much more expensive than a CD player and, physically, are much more inconvenient to use because of the size of the laser disc player and the discs. Many people predict that CD usage will far surpass laser usage in educational settings in the future.

CDS AND MULTIMEDIA

Multimedia presentations are becoming a standard method for teacher presentations, management presentations, training materials, and classroom research projects. Many programs are on the market to make authoring of multimedia presentations a relatively easy task. True multimedia combines graphics, sound, text, animation, and/or video into a single presentation. The authoring system allows multimedia creators to tie these forms of media together. Several parts of one multimedia presentation may be retrieved from CDs.

COMPUTER-BASED PRESENTATIONS

In the future, schools and businesses may create more computer-based instruction (CBI) using CDs than they have in the past. Both businesses and schools must weigh the length of creation time involved against the number of students to be trained and the cost of other training methods. Creation time for five hours of well-designed training materials in the business world may take 200 or more hours. In education, teachers may create a one-to-two hour presentation in only 20-40 hours.

Computer-based instruction (CBI) lessons can be classified into one of three types:

- drill and practice
- tutorial
- simulation.

Business educators can make use of all three types of instruction. With over 5,000 CD-ROM discs on the market and entire catalogs devoted to CDs, business educators may find titles related to the subjects they teach. Although every computer in a school may not have a CD drive at this time, future requests for bids by schools are expected to list CD-ROM capabilities as a standard requirement for all new computers purchased.

In the future CD-ROM drives will become a standard component of computers, and more application software will be sold on CDs. This technology is here to stay.

REFERENCES

Arachtingi, B. (January 1994). Tech tips: CD-Rom questions answered. *Connections.* p. 2.

Eiser, L. (April 1993). Shopping for a CD-ROM drive. *Technology & Learning.* p. 40.

Truett, C. (February 1994). CD-ROM and videodisc technology in North Carolina school library media center. *The Computing Teacher.* p. 41.

CHAPTER 16

Implications of Emerging Technologies on Business and Computer Instruction

NORMAN A. GARRETT

Eastern Illinois University, Charleston, Illinois

Computer and telecommunications technologies have brought us to a cross-road in the short history of the information revolution. Society has arrived at the point where there are so many emerging technologies that it is impossible to predict the main direction of the next changes. Clearly, the implications for educators are significant.

Thus far, some of these new technologies have not yet achieved mass appeal but have set the stage for major changes in the way technology is used in business and, hence, in the way technology is used in education. Diverse technologies such as voice recognition, wireless LANs, personal digital assistants, subnotebook computers, inexpensive but powerful scanners, and wireless modems are beginning to enter the business environment. Each has tremendous potential, both in business and in the classroom.

The purpose of this chapter is to examine some of these emerging technologies and the impact they might have on the way we do business and on the way we educate for doing business. To be sure, it takes a crystal ball to make some of these projections, especially in an industry where change occurs roughly every 18 months. However, the impact of these technologies on education cannot be underestimated, and it is instructive to examine these developments as they emerge and to plan for their possible eventual integration into the classroom environment.

CLASSROOM IMPACT

Educators rarely have the luxury of utilizing state-of-the-art technology in the classroom. There are several reasons for this.

First, in order to obtain funding, educators need to demonstrate a need for the technology. This is often accomplished by citing the way technology is used in the business world. Thus, a sequential cause and effect relationship is created, allowing educators to use only those technologies which have been proven viable, as well as commercially successful, in the workplace.

Second, budget constraints preclude educators from purchasing every technology that comes along, regardless of its potential. Educational dollars must be spent carefully to provide the most "bang for the buck." Often, this means purchasing older technologies that have been greatly reduced in price, allowing more units to be bought and more students to be served.

If society is to move forward, however, these old ways of doing things are going to have to change. The Committee on Applications and Technology, a subcommittee of the Information Infrastructure Task Force (IITF), recently published the following statement regarding the future of education and technology:

> The NII [National Information Infrastructure] brings with it a fundamental change in how information moves and is handled. In the application areas of education and commerce in particular, this change will require new ways of functioning—distinctly different from current practices—to achieve the greatest benefits from the NII. Restructuring systems and organizations to take maximum advantage of NII applications without impairing the effectiveness of the organization as a whole will require a large degree of learning and adaptation on the part of the institution. New ways of doing the job will be markedly different from past practices and may require significant investments in professional development and training because individuals (teachers for example) play key roles in these applications areas. (Committee on Applications and Technology, 1994).

Other futurists have frequently echoed these statements, saying that education will soon have to be completely revamped to accommodate new modes of conveying information. It is a certainty that the use of old budgeting paradigms to finance information technology within the framework of a new technological environment will not work at all (Sterling, 1993). Several technologies are now emerging that could have tremendous impact not only on the way we teach and convey information to students, but on the way they perceive information and gain access to it.

CONVERGENCE

The software toolbox that is currently available to us is constantly changing. Only 10 years ago, a PC user had to be a programmer to have access to many software tools. BASIC programming came with the system when you bought it, and if you wanted to do very much at all, you had to write your own programs.

Contrast that picture with today, only a few years later. Virtually anything society wants to do with the computer can be done by purchasing the appropriate software package. "User friendliness" has been achieved by encapsulating difficult-to-use software within shells that provide the user with a simpler interface and set of choices. These crude shells are only the beginning (Caudill, 1992).

Applications, as we know them, will soon cease to exist, being replaced by integrated suites of programs that can readily and rapidly communicate with each other. Rather than having to run separate programs for separate tasks, we will be able to use a collection of engines that provide text editing, math, database, messaging, and other functions. Some of these will even be integrated into the operating system of the computer (Coursey, 1994).

The user empowerment embodied in this new approach is indicative of the type of access we will all have to information, with current hardware and software converging into a single, multiple layered, "information access" interface for users. Large telecommunications corporations and conglomerates are currently positioning themselves to be able to deliver all technologies via a single digital delivery system. Voice, video, image, and data communications will be wrapped together into a single package, easy to use, and opening millions of doors to a wealth of information (Tynan, 1994).

INTERNETWORKING

One of the fundamental building blocks of the new technology will be the internetwork. An internetwork is a network of networks, with each component network being referred to as a "subnetwork." Colleges, universities, government, and many private agencies, businesses, and organizations, are tied together in an internetworking arrangement called, simply, the Internet.

While the Internet has been around for a long time, it is only now being recognized as having great potential as a teaching tool in the public schools. However, the public schools, for the most part, have lacked the funding required to connect to it.

Currently, about half the states have started to develop widespread Internet connections for schools, even though the cost per classroom connected is estimated to be as high as $5,000. (Jacobson, 1994) In spite of these efforts, it will be some time before all schools can routinely enjoy Internet connections.

But even if a classroom cannot be immediately connected directly to the Internet, it is relatively inexpensive to equip some classrooms with modems and telephone lines. Today, high speed modems (14.4 kilobytes per second transmission rates) are available for less than $200. These can be used, via standard telephone lines, to connect to many free or inexpensive bulletin boards, university computers, or even to access the Internet via a local university or college connection.

The future of education is tied closely to access to such networks. Students with access to internetworks will have a distinct advantage over students without such access, just as students today who have access to computers in the classroom have an advantage over students who do not.

One of the goals of the Information Infrastructure Task Force is to provide such access to all levels of education and to assure educators that the government will not leave education out when funding this initiative. However, educating the populace to use networks like the Internet and its successors will require that we rethink our approach to this type of learning and be open to new ideas and teaching tactics (Committee on Applications and Technology, 1994).

WIRELESS NETWORKING

Access to internetworks is only the beginning. Imagine the day, not too far off, when students can be issued a device that will automatically link them, no matter where they are physically located, to the school network and, by connection, to many other networks around the world. And imagine that this hand-held device can be put in a pocket, purse, or backpack (Bastiaens, 1993, and Pountain, 1993).

The student could arise in the morning, turn on the device, and check for school news, homework assignments, etc. Since the connection would be two-way, the student could also send messages or homework to teachers.

Such technology is currently available, albeit in an infant form. Wireless LANs work using infrared technology instead of restrictive cabling. Infrared systems are still limited to "line of sight" access, and work much the same as a TV or VCR remote control; however, they add much flexibility to local area networks (Fletcher, 1993, and Baran, 1992).

With the newly emerging cellular data networking, however, LANs can be expanded even beyond cableless infrared. Networks are currently available, for instance, that allow you to use a device called a "personal digital assistant," or PDA. When powered up, the PDA will automatically connect to a cellular data network. That network can provide access to urgent news, electronic mail, data files, and calendar and scheduling information. In addition, the PDA can accomplish many of the functions normally only done on computers such as scheduling, dialing phones, and keeping personal notes (Caruthers, 1993, and Shandle, 1992).

Currently, such technologies are expensive, due to the price of the communications links and the PDAs themselves. They are only now beginning to appear for business use, and their actual usefulness in real situations is still untested. Some PDAs use handwriting while others are keyboard based. Eventually, some type of standard will emerge (Reddy, 1994).

The benefits of such technologies are clear. For business, this extends the linkage between central data areas and remote employees in locations where wired access is not possible. Additionally, the technology allows for the development of LANs that use a similar wireless technology that enables the LAN to expand geographically beyond its characteristic local area. LANs will become "local" in logic only, while physically they may become greatly dispersed (Leonard, 1992). Although wireless LANs have many benefits, they have not been tested thoroughly for health hazards at this point.

No longer would schools using such technologies need to be wired. Classrooms and individual students could correspond electronically with each other regardless of their physical location. Students might not even be required to be physically present in the classroom in order to interact.

In business, there is a concept called "telecommuting." A telecommuter communicates with the office via a network, rather than physically going to the office. The location of the work is irrelevant, and the worker communicates and conducts business entirely by computer, going to the office infrequently for face-to-face meetings.

Imagine this concept extended to the schools. What will the classrooms of the future look like? They will likely be information centers, rather than traditional classrooms as we know them.

HAND-HELD AND PORTABLE COMPUTERS

Ten years ago, a "portable" personal computer weighed approximately 45 pounds and was the size of a large sewing machine. To carry the device, one needed to hire a large, muscular person. Then came the laptop computer. This was a much smaller computer, very limited in capacity, that weighed about 10 pounds and had a battery life of about one hour and sometimes used floppy disk drives only.

Portable computers were soon supplanted by "notebooks," that were approximately the size of a loose-leaf notebook full of paper. At first, the LCD screens were hard to read, but all that changed rapidly, and now notebook computers are light, have extended battery life, feature sharp color displays, and are just as powerful as their desktop counterparts.

The most recent development in this area has been "subnotebook" computers, or "palmtops." These are full-fledged computers with reduced-sized keyboards. Touch typing is still possible, however. They run on small AA or AAA batteries and have a battery life of about 10-20 hours. They use solid-state storage instead of hard disk, further reducing the power consumption, and they can be connected to a larger system for the transfer of data.

Educators, so far, have not adopted notebook or subnotebook computers widely. One reason has been that they have been more expensive than the same configuration in a desktop model. A second reason, however, has been security. Many schools have literally chained or bolted their desktop computers to tables to keep them from being damaged or stolen. Interestingly, this is how books were treated before the advent of printing. Libraries consisted of shelves of hand-copied books, available only to the privileged few. For security, and because of their great value, books were chained to the wall in such a way that they could be used (read) but not removed from the immediate area.

This technique was important while the books had high value. After printing was invented, however, the value of individual books dropped drastically, and they became so readily available that there was no reason to steal them or, therefore, to chain them.

Currently, computers are valuable items in many schools. As prices come down and technology becomes more affordable, perhaps there will come a day when a notebook computer is checked out to each student at the beginning of the year in much the same way as we issue textbooks now.

In the meantime, notebook computers can still be used to advantage in schools. Notebook computers are portable and yet can be used in much the same way as desktop computers. They can be attached to networks or used as standalone devices and can even be connected to wireless LANs (Fletcher, 1993).

Features for notebook computers are much the same as they are for desktop computers with the exception of hard disk capacity. This capacity will generally be lower as special hard drives must be used that are cushioned for shock and that consume less energy than standard drives.

When considering notebook or subnotebook computers for use in schools, educators should contemplate the following:

1. Notebook computers are generally more expensive than their desktop counterparts. To some extent, this difference is offset by their portability. But if portability is not an issue, stick with the desktop systems for now.

2. Extra batteries should be purchased with notebook computers. There is no standard battery, and batteries will eventually fail to hold a charge. At such time, it pays to have spare batteries that are specifically designed for the unit.

3. Even though the notebook computers are specifically designed to withstand shock, they should not be dropped. If students are going to use notebook computers, they will have to be trained on how to handle them safely.

4. Software should be legal and pre-installed on the hard drive. After student use,

extraneous files should be removed from the hard disk. This is easy to automate so that the disk is ready for use by the next student (Garrett & Lundgren, 1992).

5. If notebook computers are to be used in a limited area (like a library or classroom), measures should be taken to ensure that they are not removed. In a library, for example, this could include coding the computers so that the library security system would sound its alarm if the computers were removed from the area.

One of the great benefits to a school using notebook computers would be the ability to purchase a classroom set of computers that could be used by different classes on a rotating basis. Instead of the class going to the computer lab, the computers could be brought to the classroom for students to use at their desks. In addition, computers could be available in the library or resource center, with much the same rules as noncirculating reference works. Students could check out computers for use in the library area. This would reduce the need for staffing labs and setting aside special rooms to house computers. This procedure places the computing resource alongside the other information resources.

SCANNERS AND GRAPHIC INPUT DEVICES

Some of the most fascinating technological developments are in the area of graphics. Scanners are devices that digitize an image. Some scanning merely converts a photograph, line drawing, or other art work into digital form. With the addition of special software, scanners can be used to recognize characters and convert an image of a character to the character itself. This allows further processing of the printed material as data.

Currently, the price of scanners is well within the reach of most schools. Small hand-held scanners can scan an image up to 4-inches wide and cost as little as $100, depending upon the features desired.

Scanners allow students to select and scan graphic images, manipulate the images as they like, and integrate the images into text or graphic art. Scanners provide a mechanism for demonstrating a great degree of student creativity.

Educators considering the use of scanners should consider the following:

1. Explicit rules should be developed in regard to the scanning of copyrighted materials.

2. Scanners have many degrees of quality, ranging from the ability to scan line art only to the ability to scan full color. The size of the image on disc is directly related to the quality of the image. A simple cartoon drawing may only take 4K to store on disc, whereas a scan of a full color picture might take well in excess of a megabyte of disc storage.

3. Scanner software and the use of images is technically difficult and takes a great deal of practice.

4. For educational environments, select scanners that are versatile (i.e. ones that can scan many different resolutions and types of graphics). This provides maximum use of the scanner and allows for the greatest possible creativity.

Similar to scanners in providing digital images are digital cameras and camcorders. Digital cameras are still in the developmental stages, but they are interesting and bear watching as the prices plunge and the level of quality increases. These cameras allow the individual to take a photograph and record the photo on disc instead of on film. The image can then be transferred to the computer where it can be viewed, edited, or discarded. Once such cameras are purchased, batteries become the only necessary supplies. The discs can be reused over and over as students take more pictures.

In a similar fashion, existing camcorders can be interfaced with personal computers by installing a special board in the computer that translates the video image into digital form. Both still and full motion can be captured, although full motion uses a lot of disc space. A short video clip of only a few seconds can consume several megabytes of disc space.

In the future, these technologies are likely to merge, with digital cameras and video capture becoming a common activity among computer users. The potential uses for this type of technology in the classroom are endless.

VOICE RECOGNITION TECHNOLOGIES

An advertisement currently airs on television wherein Candace Bergen picks up a telephone and says "call home." The Sprint system recognizes her voice and automatically identifies her, looks up her home telephone number, and dials it for her. Is this reality? Yes, but with several major limitations.

Voice recognition technology has been around for some time and has primarily been used with the handicapped. The drawback of the technology has always been that the computer must "learn" the user's voice before recognition can take place. This learning process is often lengthy and usually involves only a limited vocabulary of words that can be recognized.

Recently, software developments have made voice recognition more viable. For one thing, the peripheral technologies have improved (microphones, sound boards, and faster processors), and this has made voice recognition work better. Still, though, it is relatively crude technology, and it may take decades before machines are produced that will react intelligently to any manner of human speech (O'Malley, 1993).

Products that use voice technology, although somewhat limited in their scope, have been introduced recently to the market. A television remote that uses voice activation is currently on the market and is selling well. Other products are available as well that utilize voice recognition technology, but all are characterized by the fact that they are single-purpose devices and only have to learn a small vocabulary to function (Millar, 1993).

Businesses and even court systems are beginning to investigate the use of voice recognition technologies to improve efficiency. Voice recognition, in conjunction with other technologies such as artificial intelligence, can potentially improve computer throughput and access to information (Polilli, 1992 and Hotch, 1992).

In the classroom of the future, we may see voice recognition used in much the same way we saw it used in the science fiction movies of the 1970s and 1980s. Students will be able to request information from the computer in plain English and have the information presented. The implications of this are tremendous, both in terms of the teaching approaches that could be used with such technologies, and the impact on the fabric of the curriculum itself.

Currently, it is difficult to obtain data from a computer if one cannot keyboard, read, and write. With voice recognition, the keyboard can be augmented (and possibly eventually replaced) with voice input. One software program allows computer operators to speak commands rather than using a mouse to click on icons or menus. The operator can say "File Open" instead of clicking on the words File and Open in menus. While the software works to some degree, sometimes the operator must say a word several times before the computer software understands.

Envision, in the future, a kindergartner who knows what a volcano is and who would like to see a picture of one, but who has not yet learned to read. He could simply tell the computer to show a picture of a volcano and it would appear.

For these kinds of scenarios to occur, the voice recognition technology will have to make vast improvements in the next several years. Will typing become obsolete? Probably not in the near future. But it will no longer be the sole form of input, as it has been in the past. Voice recognition, along with other visual technologies such as touch sensitive screens, will make input much less unidimensional than it has been in the past.

THE CHALLENGE

At the University of Indiana, researchers (Monaghan, 1994) are trying to develop a technological model for the classroom of the future. This model includes the use of voice recognition and other technologies, foreseeing a classroom that is actually a "sensorium," in which students would, for example, "study the passage of blood through the body—not just by reading about it, but by coursing through a simulated body themselves."

The only senses that we have been able to use to any extent thus far in the information revolution have been touch and sight. Our voice and hearing will be used next, as multimedia sound and voice recognition enter the world of personal computers. A typical personal computer can currently be upgraded, with a sound board, a microphone, and accompanying software, to recognize a limited set of voice commands and to output text as simulated speech, rather than as a display on a monitor. And this is only the beginning of the usage of such technologies. One can only imagine the kinds of instruction that teachers could create when armed with such tools.

Clearly, technology changes so rapidly that it is difficult to keep track of developments. Educators need to be farsighted and look at longer term trends and their possible impact on the current paradigm of American education. PDAs, internetworking, and wireless networks are already here. Virtual reality technologies using sight, sound, touch, and hearing are within sight. As the recent movie *Disclosure* showed, the user interface of the immediate future may be visual. To locate a file, a computer operator may walk down a "virtual reality" hallway, choose an office to enter, proceed to open a file cabinet, browse through file folders visually, pull out a file folder, and read the file contents on the computer screen.

While these developments are amazing and almost seem like science fiction, are we ready for them as educators? Do we have the educational infrastructure to accommodate the new technologies in new learning styles?

is to begin to think about the reshaping that must be done
nts develop appropriate learning behaviors for the 21st
yond so that they may take their places in a world about which
dream.

REFERENCES

Antonoff, M. (April 1992). Next generation PCs. *Popular Science.* p. 70-75.

Baran, N. (April, 1992). Wireless networking. *Byte.* p. 291-294.

Bastiaens, G. (November 22, 1993). The future of the PDA. *Electronic Design.* p. 43.

Caruthers, F. (May 1993). Networking: Wireless datacom sparks mobile revolution. *Computer Design.* p. OEM11-OEM18.

Caudill, M. (April 1992). Kinder, gentler computing. *Byte.* p. 134-140.

Committee on Applications and Technology, Information Infrastructure Task Force. What it takes to make it happen: Key issues for applications of the national information infrastructure. Paper published January 25, 1994.

Coursey, D. (February 1994). A whole lot of converging goin' on. *PC World.* p. 47.

Fletcher, P. (September 27, 1993). Wireless LAN adapter fits into PCMCIA card. *Electronics.* p. 11.

Garrett, N., and Lundgren, T. (Spring, 1992). Microcomputer laboratory management. *Journal of Microcomputer Systems Management.* p. 13-20.

Hotch, R. (May 1992). Computers find their voice. *Nation's Business.* p. 49.

Jacobson, R. (February 2, 1994). Connecting the schools. *The Chronicle of Higher Education.* p. A17-A18.

Leonard, M. (March 19, 1992). Wireless data links broaden LAN options. *Electronic Design.* p. 51-52.

Millar, H. (May 3, 1993). At least the TV might listen to you. *Business Week.* p. 160.

Monaghan, P. (March 2, 1994). Sensoriums and virtual textbooks. *The Chronicle of Higher Education.* p. A27-A29.

O'Malley, C. (May 1993). Voice recognition gets real. *Popular Science.* p. 74-77.

Polilli, S. (September 1992). The high-tech court of the future. *Governing.* p. 18-19.

Pountain, D. (October 1993). "PDA CPUs: New form demands new functions. *Byte.* p. 80-81.

Reddy, S. (February 1994). Roam free: wireless networking with AirShare and AirAccess. *PC Computing.* p. 62-64.

Shandle, J. (April 1992). Wireless LANs: Welcome to the virtual workplace. *Electronics.* p. 26.

Sterling, B. (May 10, 1993). You asked for it, you got it. Speech at National Academy of Sciences Convocation on Technology and Education, Washington D.C.

Tynan, D. (February 1994). PC meets TV. *PC World.* p. 137-147.

TECHNOLOGY IN THE CLASSROOM